Praise for *Abandoning*

"They say that art is where you find it, and René McMillen finds a lot of it in small town America. She makes the case that the art world extends far beyond the hubs of New York and Los Angeles, and highlights artists who are experts in their craft in the small communities they love. An inspiration for anyone blessed (cursed?) with artistic ability, René shows there are lots of appreciative audiences for an artist's work."

—Dave Lerner, retired TV anchor
and newscaster, and writer

"Reading René McMillen's *Abandoning the Road to Hollywood: How to Thrive as an Artist in Your Community*, made me realize that although I haven't written a book that's landed on the best-seller list, I can still be proud of what I have written, and that my creativity is mine to own and not based on monetary success."

—Merissa Racine, stenographer by day
and author of *Silent Gavel*

"Through the seamless retelling of life events, McMillen creates an immensely personal connection for artists of any medium on their path—to publication, recitation, performance, or gallery space. A self-confessed 'searching artist,' McMillen's journey isn't built on gathering the most likes, followers, or comments. Rather, the Wyoming artist's vocation began simply with a belief that she was an artist. From that belief, she pioneered a path to bring creativity into her life and her rural West community. There are so many gems in *Abandoning the Road to Hollywood: How to Thrive as an Artist in Your Community*, you'll find yourself reaching for a highlighter, dog-earing a page of the book, or texting a quote to a fellow artisan."

—Mary Biliter, Art Education Specialist at Wyoming
Arts Council by day and author of seventeen books

ABANDONING
THE ROAD
TO HOLLYWOOD

RENÉ C. MCMILLEN

ABANDONING THE ROAD TO HOLLYWOOD

How to Thrive as an Artist in Your Community

Shelle—
So love your heart &
desire for excellance!
May you flourish where
you are planted!

Reni M'Millen

TriForce Publishing
3959 Van Dyke Road, Suite 265
Lutz, FL 33558
TriForcePublishing.com

Cover design by JT Lindroos

ISBN: 1-64396-205-1
ISBN-13: 978-1-64396-205-4

TABLE OF CONTENTS

You are creative. You are damn creative. Each and every one of you. You are so much more creative than all the other dry, boring morons that you work with.
—Michael, *The Office*

Introduction

The warm sun had already slipped below the horizon on a cold day in 1993. I parked behind the U-Haul along a dark street on the edge of town. As I unstrapped my three-month-old daughter from her car seat, the wind shook the silver Chevy. With the baby's head covered with a white flannel blanket to protect her from the December breeze, I hurried into the small house we had rented in Cheyenne, Wyoming. Despite the dark paneled walls and the green shag carpeted floor, I mustered up hope at our new start for my husband, two-year-old son, Ethan, and new baby, Savannah.

I never imagined I would live in Cheyenne. Ever. It wasn't even on my top twenty places to visit list. It's not a dream destination. Cheyenne, a town settled among the prairie grass and sage brush, was a place I drove through on my way to somewhere else. But it was close to my family, and my husband and I wanted to join a new church in Cheyenne.

The church modeled its weekend services after another church in Chicago which used the arts. As I became more involved in planning music, drama, and media for the church, I questioned: Where are we going to find artists? We are in Cheyenne, WYOMING!! Not an artist's mecca like Chicago, Hollywood, Nashville, or New York City. After a few announcements during the church service asking for volunteers to act or create a PowerPoint with pictures and music (which we called medias), or sing, people popped up like antelope in the scrubby sage.

Like myself, the volunteers didn't think they were artists, but would give acting, or singing, or creating medias a try. There was a former bull rider turned roof contractor who acted in dramas, a retail manager who directed the dramas, and a construction supervisor who staged the drama props. A mail carrier sang, a middle school teacher strummed guitar, and a nurse played piano in the band. A pediatrician configured lights for the stage, an auto mechanic mixed the sound board, and a financial analyst put together song slides on PowerPoint. There was a mom of six kids who created medias, a store display stylist who painted with oils, and a music teacher who wrote songs. As time went on, I discovered not only were there artists in Cheyenne, but there were gifted, talented, and exceptional artists in this cowpoke town of fifty thousand souls.

The challenge was none of the volunteers saw themselves as *real* artists. Most knew they would never use their creative skills beyond Cheyenne. All had "real" jobs and fit the creativity in the small gaps of their busy lives. And because they were never going to be famous artists, they didn't take their creative gifts seriously.

Beginning in 1995, as I became fully invested in the artists within the church, I made another discovery. Our community of a hundred artists had affected and enhanced the perspectives of thousands of local people. These artists, who were never going to have their names on Broadway, or perform on the Grand Ole Opry stage, contributed to the positive personal growth of people in the Cheyenne area. Yes, we were way off Broadway (1846 miles to be exact!), but we were still important to our local community's culture.

And these artists impacted my own artist's journey. For thirteen years as we collaborated on creative projects and explored outside the box of "normal" church services, I discovered my artistic gifts too. As I became an advocate for their artist journey, they pulled me to discover my own artist's path. Even after I left my position as creative director, the artistic fire within me wouldn't, or couldn't, die. I continued to stumble along the journey attempting to understand and fully live out what it means to thrive as an artist in my community.

Who are you to write a book about artists? I have asked myself many, many times while writing and rewriting. My answer: A nobody. I'm just a woman who worked with and encouraged small-town artists for twenty-six years. No degree in the fine arts. No book on the New York Times bestseller list. No interview with Jimmy Fallon. To some people, this makes me unqualified to write to artists about creativity because I haven't made it BIG. There are many artists who have made it BIG and have written about their journey to stardom. I've read their books!

However, not making it BIG doesn't mean I've lived a *small* artist's life. I may be an average woman, but I'm BIG on encouraging creative identity and mission. I talk LOUDLY to fears and doubts to be the best artist I can be. I understand the COLOSSAL challenge of communicating to the uncreative world at the risk of being misunderstood. I deal with a JUMBO sized package of highly sensitive emotions. And I've experienced the MONUMENTAL contributions of artists to their neighborhood or city.

Through my artistic birth and growth and the stories of artists I've met along the way, I attempt to examine the challenges of the artist's journey within the local communities we live in. This book addresses the necessity of the artist's awakening to his or her creative gifts and the commitment to nurturing the artist within. Each chapter is written on a topic that came from listening to artists and is framed by a creative element such as painting, music, literature, film, theater, etc. And because I'm an average person, this book also tells the stories of other average people living BIG in their creative dreams.

My aspiration is that, like many of the artists in this book, you will discover your creativity, commit to your art, and grow beyond your most outlandish dream.

My dream is for you to take this book, dog-ear the corners, underline motivational thoughts, doodle in the margins, and pass it on to the next undiscovered artist.

My hope is that you will overcome fears and thrive as an artist right where you are experiencing life.

Share your story at rcmcmillen.com.

The artist is the person who makes life more interesting or beautiful, more understandable or mysterious, or probably in the best sense, more wonderful.
—George Bellows, painter

Chapter 1
Painting a Self-Portrait

I. Can. Not. Stop. Looking. At. Him.

The light from the ceiling track cylinders animate both the color and shape of his face. A buoyant tuft of orange-red hair floats above his creamy white forehead. His prominent long nose hangs on his thin face. Stern with concentration, his lips flatten to a narrow line. As I focus on his steel blue eyes, they seem to squint at me, as if he is memorizing the contours of my face.

I lean in closer. I notice the many brushstrokes creating his beard. There are dashes of cinnamon brown, creamy yellow, and ginger orange. I inspect the portrait background surrounding his face. A variety of blue shades comprise the backdrop of the portrait. I count seven bristles imprinted in one sweep of thick sapphire blue oil paint, which captures the touch of an artist looking for his place, his stroke, his voice.

I step back and take in the full view of Vincent van Gogh's self-portrait. I wonder what he would say to me, a searching artist. At the moment, I hear nothing from Vincent, but rather a deep male voice giving me insights, through my earphones, into van Gogh's life as an artist. For two hours, my sixteen-year-old daughter and I wander around a large room in a museum along with hundreds of other people to survey the works of van Gogh's traveling art display. People jockey by me, as I stare, listen and embrace the emotion of van Gogh's self-perception formed by his childhood.

Van Gogh picked up paintbrushes as a child and took a few lessons. But when he came to the age to determine his life's vocation, he studied theology and prepared to be a clergyman. Because of his deep compassion for the poor, the church sent him to a parish that served an impoverished community. After only six months, the church rejected him, saying he lacked communication skills. Searching for renewed identity and purpose, van Gogh daringly grabbed his paintbrushes.

In our journey through life, the pursuit of our self-identity is always our most heroic act.

I assume a hero is superhuman, like Supergirl or Spiderman, who does courageous acts such as saving both his girlfriend and a cable car with kids dangling from a bridge. Or I picture a hero as a brave firefighter who jumps into scorching fires to rescue people or animals trapped in a burning structure. To behave in a heroic way doesn't require wearing a cape (though I am braver when I do!). Heroism isn't merely an outward act, but it can be an inner undertaking of scraping back the layers of who we are.

It takes courage to remove our personal masquerade and discover the natural gifts and talents which may differ from those of our parents, siblings or friends. It takes bravery to pioneer a unique path which may separate us from the expectations of family and friends. Only self-discovery can allow us to go beyond the limitations imposed by self or others and lead us from the ordinary to the extraordinary.

OMG! I'm an Artist?

Years ago, as I approached adulthood, I studied at various theological colleges, developing a love for the sacred and those poor in spirit. I went to Alaska to serve in remote villages and considered living in Alaska as a missionary. But I received an evaluation by my supervisor who concluded my extraverted personality didn't fit the introverted culture of the Last Frontier. Undaunted, I continued looking for my place, bounced around working in different capacities, and landed as a creative director. The church leaders bravely commissioned me and my teams to use the arts in the services. This wasn't the traditional way of doing church. No hymnals or overhead projectors were harmed or used. Instead, a film clip would begin the service to pose a question, two actors portrayed a scene from life wrestling with the question, then a song would give the audience time to reflect before the pastor would speak. Then the next week, we would change it up. No weekend services were the same. The attendees never knew what was going to happen. It was risky. It was controversial. And it was exhilarating.

To succeed in my job and grow in my leadership abilities, I devoured books like *Good to Great*, by Jim Collins, and *Developing the Leader Within You*, by John C. Maxwell. To connect with the artists, I savored *The Heart of the Artist*, by Rory Noland, and *The Artist's Way* by Julia Cameron. Always on the hunt for a new book to motivate and encourage artists, I found one which not only affected them, but me too.

Every week for two months, five of us met and discussed each chapter in *The Creative Call*, by Janice Elsheimer. One activity asked us to document our creativity during childhood. When I looked back and scanned my personal terrain with an artist's lens, I discovered an identity I thought I had forgotten.

Many of my childhood memories contained creative activities.

Whether it was with ink, music, fabric, paint, film, flour, or flowers, I loved dreaming something new for other people to enjoy. When I was fifteen years old and making your own clothes was popular, I changed the collar and added puffy sleeves to my dress design. When I was eighteen, after a hike with my camera in the Rocky Mountains, I took the images and made them into notecards as gifts for others. In my early twenties, I played "The Wedding March" on the piano, "The Wedding Song" on the guitar, and "Jesu, Joy of Man's Desiring" on the flute at a wedding. In my young mind, I considered myself creative, but not an artist.

From my youthful perspective, the idea of an artist conjured up images of a bankrupt painter gaunt with hunger, or a temperamental musician dressed in Picasso-like clothing. An artist wouldn't live in Wyoming, or any small community. I assumed a true artist would live in one of the creative hubs like Santa Fe, Atlanta, or Seattle.

As I recovered these creative childhood memories, my heart remembered the excitement and energy of those activities. My soul relived the pleasure of picking up developed photos (that's right—pictures came from 35mm film, not your snazzy iPhone), laying them out on the table, and being thrilled at what my creative eye and camera lens captured.

Until age twenty-six, my days sparkled with bursts of creativity. But somewhere along the adult pathway, my inventive nature was buried under the grown-up responsibilities of work, family obligations, and societal expectations. My creative nature was all but forgotten until I scraped back a few layers of my busy life.

I compared Elsheimer's definition of an artist to my memories of creativity. The two paralleled and implied that I was an artist. I had never considered myself as an artist. And no one ever called me an artist. I couldn't quite accept that I was an artist, but the possibility of this identity bridged my past to the present. Years of creativity had prepared me to lead other creatives. If I was an artist too, how would my new awareness impact my creative director job?

After eight years of cultivating and experiencing an artistic community, my management abilities and teams were thriving. My leadership went from being unsure and passive to clear and guiding. I felt like I was leading a revolution with artists who challenged the audience to see old, tired stories in new ways.

Within the artists' groups, a positive and safe culture flourished and allowed them to explore their creativity. Week by week, new and meaningful art kept me mesmerized. The imaginations and originality of a small community of creatives in Wyoming caused me to question my assumptions of where artists existed.

I had found my place in a creative community in rural Wyoming. Even though the job demanded much from my whole being, I thrived on the thrill of encouraging other artists. My creativity surged at flood level and I envisioned myself being in the job for a long time. But it was not to be.

Leadership at the church changed, the new pastor made an unexpected move in my job description, and I was out looking for work. The loss of my artist job left me with a deep sense of rejection and loss.

I spent the next eight years existing like a misfit toy on a freezing island while working in the financial sector and in city government. In the midst of those who effortlessly rolled as money counters, I appeared to be like the squared-wheeled train toy. In the complicated sea of paper-pushers, I was the boat who couldn't keep afloat. Like the misfit toy elephant with dots, there was a love-hate relationship that made me both different and unique. No matter how hard I tried, I didn't fit in. I didn't thrive. The effort to be someone I wasn't produced mental and physical exhaustion. The false self I maintained almost muted the bright hues of my creative personality. In an attempt to save myself, I jumped off the whirly-swirly corporate enclave.

In hindsight, my mismatched abilities in the corporate culture not only altered my direction but corrected my journey. I could have sought another office job, but knew it wasn't in my cache of talents or interests. Van Gogh could have pursued employment with another church.

But leaving that behind defined his artist's life. Although his empathies for the poor and the church remained, as seen in his paintings *The Sower at Sunset*, *Starry Night*, and others, his path was redirected and devoted to the artist's life.

Imposter Portraits

Perhaps my inability to recognize my artistic nature results from growing up in the rural West. I wasn't exposed to art galleries. I didn't have opportunities to hear symphonies or attend the theater. In my community, pursuing a career in the arts was unreasonable and absurd. But the barren artistic landscape couldn't deaden the creative quality hard-wired into my being.

Often, when seeking our artistic identity, we permit others to paint our portrait. We allow them to add color and shape according to what they think is important. With the best intentions, they warn us that pursuing an artist's life is irrational and won't generate sufficient income. They may highlight many of our characteristics, but they may not clearly comprehend some of our inner attributes and passions.

To avoid controversy, criticism, or isolation, many of us paint our portrait by taking identity cues from others. Rather than exploring our own abilities and thoughts, we monitor what others do and say. We then copy their expectations onto our canvas, creating a false image of who we are.

Pretending to be someone we aren't instigates a clash between the false self and our true identity. The false image thrives on the praise and applause from significant others and suppresses our real character, leaving the true self to battle for survival. Eventually the pressure of the war causes the false image to crack and flake off. The true self seeps between the cracks and pours itself over the canvas.

While it may seem easiest to paint your portrait with a paint-by-number kit, it's not. It's quite exhausting. Impersonating a money-counting, number-touting, rule-abiding employee took enormous energy. My artistic nature fought for survival and won.

Near the end of the van Gogh exhibit, the recorded tour tells how they found the artist in a field with blood on his head—a discreet description for children taking the self-guided tour. Van Gogh's early death was a tragedy, not only for his family, but also for the unrealized potential of his creativity. For me, van Gogh's emotional torment and suicide symbolize the forfeited quest of any artist searching for their identity.

I Dare You to Boldly Sign Your Portrait!

Step by step, the museum tour takes us art enthusiasts through van Gogh's skill progression of sketches and early paintings. As I observe his first charcoal drawings, I note nothing spectacular. *I can draw like that.* But with each picture, I notice his bold and bright technique evolving and forming.

Besides van Gogh's self-portrait, one painting stands out from the rest. Entitled *Seascape at Saintes-Maries,* it depicts a fishing ship nearly drowning in the stormy waves. The blue-black hues of thick oil paint capture the depth of the tumultuous waves. In the left-hand corner, in red paint, van Gogh signed his name: *Vincent.* Not his last name which is traditional in art, not with dark paint, which is common among painters, but in the most vibrant blood-red in the color wheel. Through my earphones I'm told that van Gogh only signed in red if he was pleased with his paint creation. It wasn't commonplace for him to do so. And only a handful of his paintings have a red signature.

I point at van Gogh's signature and ask my daughter, "What kind of artist signs a painting in red?" She shrugs and keeps walking through the tour. I pause, survey Vincent's signature one last time, and smile at the bold act of identification.

My self-identity is multidimensional: I am female, an American with a Spanish and Scottish heritage, and a Western cultural influence from growing up on a ranch. This is the identity which appears on the surface and others quickly see. Yet, I am more than my gender or nationality.

At one time I identified myself as a church servant, musician, wife, mother, and leader. Those are the roles I have played. But who I am, behind those outward acts, is an artist. While I didn't realize it at the time, my artistic identity still infused all the dimensions of my existence.

For me, the recognition of my artistic identity came about more like an impressionistic painting rather than an instantly produced Polaroid. First, brushstrokes of childhood exploration played over the canvas. Dabs of musical performances, journal writing, and handmade gifts were layered on the adolescence background. Thick wavy lines of photography sweep to the edges of the canvas. Up close, one sees only the strokes of activity which appear random and aimless. It's not until stepping back and viewing the whole scene that the innumerable strokes merge to create a self-portrait of an artist. And being pleased, I can boldly sign in red.

Dreams and Infinity

An artist is a person who not only admires color, design, form, words, music, etc., but also desires to create something out of those elements. Our imagination foresees a design, and our creativity gives birth to an original art piece. Artists are those of us who see what is and dream about what can be. We see a musical instrument and our mind hears the melody. We see a garden and our brush paints the flowers on canvas. We see a blank page and imagine the story.

The awareness of your artistic nature doesn't mean you've finished the self-portrait. You've only started the charcoal outline of your identity. There are more creative hopes which will add hues of shading to the painting. There will be brave and courageous and heroic aspects of your self-discovery which will add depth. As van Gogh wrote in a letter to his brother Theo (Van Gogh Museum, *The Letters to Theo van Gogh*, Arles, Saturday, August 18, 1888, http://www.vangoghletters.org/vg/letters/let663/letter.html#translation)

"I should like to paint the portrait of an artist friend who dreams great dreams, who works as the nightingale sings, because it is his nature. This man will be fair-haired. I should like to put my appreciation, the love I have for him, into the picture. So I will paint him as he is, as faithfully as I can—to begin with. But that is not the end of the picture. To finish it, I shall be an obstinate colourist. I shall exaggerate the fairness of the hair, arrive at tones of orange, chrome, pale yellow. Behind the head—instead of painting the ordinary wall of the shabby apartment, I shall paint infinity, I shall do a simple background of the richest, most intense blue that I can contrive, and by this simple combination, the shining fair head against this rich blue background, I shall obtain a mysterious effect, like a star in the deep blue sky."

As your artist's self-portrait evolves and forms, I encourage you to take van Gogh's painting advice: faithfully paint yourself as a dreamer of great dreams and give yourself the mysterious effect of a shining star.

I haven't painted a self-portrait. It's on my to-do list. But I have painted, with my imagination, a picture of the artist I want to be. And even then, it's not easy to paint myself as a dreamer. Often, I paint myself dimly lit in the confines of a shabby apartment. No infinity.

No shining glow to myself.

Comprehending that I am an artist comes with a huge sense

of relief and peace. I can put away the false identity and move forward as a creative person. Embracing my identity as an artist solved which of the multiple life roads to pursue. What I didn't realize was the artist's journey comes with its own set of challenges, a designated-for-the-artist-path kind of obstacles. Not the ordinary pitfalls that occur in all life paths like corporate ladder climbing and health care coverage, but the kind of sinkholes that cause you to pause and think about foregoing the artist call and go back to the shabby apartment.

Use the following questions to prompt reflection and self-discovery on your own artist's journey.

The Artist's Palette

1. What is your definition of an artist?
2. Do you think you are an artist? Why? Why not?
3. Is your public self-portrait a true representation of your inner passions?
4. Could you sign your portrait in bold red paint?
5. What fears do you have about being an artist?
6. Using van Gogh's suggestions, gather together other artist friends and paint a self-portrait.

Creativity takes courage.
—Henri Matisse

Chapter 2
The Creative Underground

As I enter the front door of the tattoo studio, I face a three-by-four-foot gold-framed painting of a female dancer. She is dressed in a delicate white tutu, performing a deep curtsy while looking up at her audience with large round eyes, one blackened and bruised. It's both beautiful and haunting. *What caused her black eye?* Pulling my eyes from the fascinating portrait, I follow the bright white fluorescent lights around a partial white wall to see two office spaces divided by waist-high wood partitions. Each space has a black ink bed covered in clear plastic and various tools and bottles on adjacent counters. It looks clean. It smells clean.

The resident artist and owner of the tattoo shop walks out from a back doorway and gives me a firm handshake, "I'm Shane Ingram."

He is dressed in jeans and a black short-sleeved T-shirt exposing his colorful tattooed arm. Shane, who is in his late thirties, gives me an inquiring eye, "So what are you writing about?"

I had phoned him two days ago asking for an interview for a book I was writing about artists for artists. I sit down on an old blue-and-green flowered couch, grab the pen clipped to my notebook, and find a clean page. "You did a beautiful tattoo on my son and I really admired the artistry. So I am curious about your story as an artist."

Shane lifts his Monster drink and takes two swigs. Setting the drink on the spotless counter, Shane begins, "I remember drawing from the moment I could hold a pencil. I sketched people, pets, and landscapes, everything I could see."

Drawing brought a deep satisfaction to Shane, and soon friends and family noticed his artistic ability. When Shane was fourteen, a friend admired a few of Shane's sketches on paper, and asked him to draw on flesh—to create a tattoo.

Shane was reluctant. Sketching on flat, hard, nonporous paper had to be different than sketching on round, soft, porous skin. Fears filled Shane's mind: *What if his tattoo looked more like a kitten than a tiger? What if this friend, aka tattoo guinea pig, is disappointed, or even angry, at the results of a botched tattoo?*

The friend assured Shane of his trust in Shane's skills. So, Shane put needle to flesh and began his next drawing. Then another person asked Shane to create a tattoo. And then another.

Shane's mom, who fully supported his artistic pursuits, ordered Shane's first tattoo kit from a website. While most high school students worked at local fast food places, Shane worked his art into a business.

Shane's artistic success prompted him to look at attending art school after high school graduation. Most of his peers planned to attend the local university, but Shane recognized his path was veering in another direction. He knew he was an artist and had to invest in his passion for drawing. After researching options, Shane attended Art Instruction School in Minneapolis, Minnesota—the same institute where Charles Schulz, the creator of the *Peanuts* cartoon, trained as an illustrator. Shane courageously left the safe path, the security of the navigated trail, and chose to traverse the little known and wild frontier of tattoo artistry.

Navigating the Tunnels of Fear and Doubt

There is the well-worn path of life which is comfortable and predictable. We're pretty sure we won't get lost. Most go to college, get an entry-level job, work their way up the pay scale, get a mortgage, and regularly add to their IRA funds. No big surprises and few variations occur along this busy road. Oh, there is the occasional layoff, or job change, but most reengage with a similar job in another building or city. The well-worn path has heavy traffic and the end destination is known. It's safe. It's common. It's Plan A.

Yet for artists, the originality of our vision and passion leads us through more twists and turns of life's path. We have to decide whether to go to a regular college, go to a specific art institute, or find an internship in the art community. The artist's path is unpredictable with more surprises. We wonder if we will get a job related to our art that will pay for rent and student loans. *And what is an IRA?* Not only is the destination evolving, but we experience more bumps on the unfamiliar road. We encounter Plan B—no, Plan C…okay, Plan K—because the path isn't set; it changes, or we get lost and become unsure of what's next. As an artist, doubts about our abilities, and fears of the unknown, can suck us into the dark tunnels of the creative underground where we stagnate and remain unproductive.

Over the years, I have been interested in many different activities: gardening, wine, roses, running, photography, spirituality, hiking, writing, books, painting, movies, baking, Impressionist art, antique furniture, and McCoy pottery. I would flirt with two or three or five of my interests. I would research the subject, get excited, and submerge my mind and heart into that activity.

I have loved photography since I was young, entering my images in the county fair, buying different cameras, printing my images and giving them as gifts. I didn't spend money to take a photography class, nor to learn the photo-editing software I purchased. Instead, I would get frustrated because my images didn't have the extraordinary touch I was hoping for. I would become disheartened from unsuccessful attempts to use the editing software. Then I would get diverted to another artistic interest and start focusing on it. The whole cycle would begin again: research, purchases, trying to create art, dissatisfaction, and jumping to another subject. I learned a lot from dabbling in different art forms, but I longed for focus and sustained fulfillment.

I felt stuck, spinning in place and looping the same results. I prayed: *What is my purpose on earth?* I became introspective: *What are my best gifts?* I talked to other artists: *How did they choose their primary art form?* I read books on success: *Could fear and perfectionism be the underlying cause of my lack of traction?*

Beneath my artistic dabbling lay a dark labyrinth of tunnels filled with doubts and fears about being an artist. Fears of failure, change, poverty, and rejection kept me lost, trapped, and meandering along dim channels. Fear fooled my artistic navigation; its pungent fumes dulled my imagination and disoriented my soul.

Our fears may come from a belief that has nothing to do with our artistic gifts. A people pleaser, a person who puts others ahead of his or her own needs, operates by the fear of rejection and failure. They believe that if they keep everyone happy, they won't be rejected. If they follow what others desire, they won't fail. You can see how this behavior would imprison an artist, crippling their creativity.

The limits of our creativity are defined by the doubts and fears in our mind. Doubt beckons me to play it safe. Doubt tells me it's too scary to be an artist and it's better to stay comfortable and walk the worn trail. Fear condemns my creative energy. Fear hyper-critiques my art and devalues my artistic influence on the world. To find my way out of the creative underground of fears and doubts, I began by examining the negative messages my mind was sending.

Although fear burrows deep within my mind, I don't have to succumb to the frightful echoes within the tangle of underground tunnels. Whenever doubt mocks my creations, I counter it with truth: *I am a developing artist with much more to learn. Take a risk, grow from it. It doesn't need to be perfect to be beautiful, emotional, or interesting.* From those positive messages, courage finds its way into my being. I acknowledge the doubts but choose to trek the artist's adventure anyway.

I defy the fears by identifying them: *What am I really afraid of? Is it ridicule? Or is it failure? Why am I scared? Am I feeling unworthy or insecure?* With every adrenaline rush of fear, I douse it with faith and conviction.

A lifestyle of faith—a perspective that conveys that there is a purpose for my art—is the exit from the tunnels of fears and doubts. As an author, I bravely work by faith. I sit at my computer and type words into paragraphs and pages. There is no guarantee the energy I spend choosing words will influence anyone. Yet, I believe in myself and the words. While I haven't seen any results, I hope for an audience who will be encouraged by these words.

Faith can be in God who is Himself creative. I'm aware that you, the reader, may not have the same faith in a Supreme God as I do, but I hope you believe in Someone bigger than yourself. It's what gives hope that our art has a larger purpose and benefits humanity. For me, faith in God and in myself is the doorway out of the maze of fear and doubt. Oh, they may voice their opinions; I will never be rid of them. But they don't have to direct my creativity or artistic goals.

When I would normally lean toward safety, protecting my ego and creative craft from criticism, I choose risk instead. I decide to be honest and vulnerable in my writing and allow other writers to proof my chapters. When I am hypercritical of my work, I tell myself that I am satisfied with the process of creating, knowing I can improve. Replacing the nagging messages of fear and doubt renews the mind and influences the art I create. In defying fear, I have the courage and freedom to nurture my artistic life aboveground, in the sunshine, for the benefit of others.

While we must do the inner work of believing in ourselves, knowing someone who's gone before us in an art career can also help dispel fears and doubts, and gives courage and confidence in our artistic journey.

Guidance Out of the Dark Tunnels

I ask Shane about his doubts and fears as an artist.

"I face many fears as owner of a tattoo studio in a small town," Shane says as he looks out the front window of his store. "There are the challenges of paying wages, licensing fees, and commercial space rent. And then there are the doubts of finding quality artist employees, and the frustration of dealing with rival studios doing cheap tattoos. And the rejection by a few business owners can really mess with your confidence."

As quickly as he names the challenges, he assures me, "But every day, I get to do what I love!"

Shane continually strives to get to the next level as an artist. He still sketches an hour every day. And he readily admits that many of his fears as an artist are overcome by having a mentor.

After attending the Art Instruction School in Minnesota, Shane searched for the best tattoo artist in the local area and asked to be mentored. Todd Trevekis, who currently owns a tattoo parlor a couple of streets over, hired Shane as an apprentice. Under Todd's mentorship, Shane learned about tattoo techniques and business savvy. He watched as Todd dealt with customers and created excellent art. Gregg Skibo, another tattoo business owner, also encouraged Shane to attend a local college to complete his degree in the fine arts. A few years ago, Shane left his mentor and started the Rotton Apple Ink Tattoo and Piercing Shop. Because his mentor had skillfully led him through the fears and challenges of being an artist and owning a business, Shane had the courage to do the same. He became a mentor to Matt, another art student. While Shane coaches about art and business, they also share creative ideas, spur each other to become better artists, and give encouragement for the artistic pilgrimage.

Which mentors helped me on my artist's journey? I check off a mental list which includes a high school music teacher who encouraged my piano playing. Also on the list are a few professors who gave me high marks and positive comments on my papers and thesis. But I've never spent a significant amount of time in the physical presence of a mentor. Instead, my mentors are authors who write about art and self-awareness. Authors such as Julie Cameron, Mary Pipher, Annie Dillard, and Virginia Woolf have influenced my ideas about art, writing, and womanhood. When I have a question about writing, or I am feeling discouraged in my artist's journey, I finger through my bookshelf asking one of the ladies for help. As I flip through the pages of the book *Writing to Change the World,* Mary Pipher advises me to write with passion. Or Annie Dillard in her book *Bird by Bird*, warns me that perfectionism "will ruin your writing, blocking inventiveness and playfulness and life force" (p.28). Virginia Woolf continues to embolden me, beyond her death, to find my voice and creative space as a female writer. Without these mentors, and many I haven't mentioned, fear and doubt would trap me in the bowels of the creative underground.

As I gather my notebook and purse and stand up to leave, Shane asks, "What are your artistic dreams? What are you hoping to achieve with your writing, with your repurposed furniture business?"

He listens intently as my hopes for the book and the dreams for my business bubble out of me. He invites me to the monthly artist tour; tells me how energizing it is to be with other artists and enjoy their art. He offers space in his tattoo studio to display my painted furniture. We shake hands, and I walk toward the front door.

I pause again to admire the impressive painting of the black-eyed dancer. When I first viewed her an hour ago, I wondered if she was a statement for victims of abuse. But now, after experiencing Shane's artistic journey, and reflecting on my personal labyrinth of fears, I wonder if the bruised eye occurred from pursuing her art.

What if the injury came from trying a new and complicated choreography and she stumbled? I imagine her trying over and over, with doubt and fear as her dancing partners, and falling.

Because I first focused on the discolored eye, I didn't notice there was also a sense of satisfaction in her face, a hint of a smile on her lips. Perhaps she has a mentor who supports her artist's heart and coaches her through the difficult steps. It's possible her black eye is a badge of courage for battling through her doubts. Maybe the black-eye symbolizes her determination and no quit attitude as she accomplishes the demanding dance. It could be she is a black-eyed heroine who defies fear and joyfully finishes with a curtsy and a smile.

Reflect on the following questions to move from the underground of fear into the light of courage and freedom.

Excavating the Underground

1. What fears do you experience about being an artist?
2. What doubts do you experience about your art?
3. Shane took steps to improve himself as an artist like going to college and finding a mentor. What steps do you need to take to become the best artist you can be?
4. Do you have a mentor? Who can you ask to be your mentor?
5. Find a "mantra for courage." Choose one to overcome your fears and doubts? Would you get it as a tattoo?
6. Listen and watch "Two Steps from Hell" by Heart of Courage on YouTube
   https://www.youtube.com/watch?v=XYKUeZQbMF0
7. Have you identified a purpose for your art?

The two most important days in your life are the day you are born, and the day you find out why.
—Mark Twain

Chapter 3
Pursuing a Mission from God

A pile of hardwood crackles in the fireplace to warm the family room on this cold winter evening. My three grade-school age kids nestle on the brown leather couches, contently crunching on buttery popcorn. I flip through the TV channels searching for something good to watch. I land on a channel showing a nun using a yardstick to slap two large men sitting in student desks, for their "bad attitudes and filthy mouths." The kids and I laugh at the comical mischievousness of two men, dressed in black suits and wearing black sunglasses, as they try to escape a nun's punishing blows. Checking the TV channel menu, I discover we are watching the 1980 movie *The Blues Brothers*. I don't remember why, but I failed to see *The Blues Brothers* on the big screen. I was in college in the 80s, living the life of term papers and ramen noodles. Instead, twenty years later, in a most timely manner, I happen upon this classic movie.

The late-night TV show *Saturday Night Live* has produced many successful comedians, including the duo of Dan Aykroyd and John Belushi. As cast members on *SNL*, they were innovative and outrageous, quickly becoming audience favorites. A musical sketch about a pair of singing brothers, Joliet Jake and Elwood Blues, appeared three times on *SNL*. Its crowd-pleasing antics of crazy dance moves and blues music took on a life of its own with concerts, an album, and a film, *The Blues Brothers*.

In the film, Aykroyd and Belushi play two criminal brothers who set out to legally raise money to save their childhood home, a Catholic orphanage. The old sage janitor encourages the brothers to go to church—it would help them change their deviant ways. The church service, led by singer James Brown, is animated with singing and dancing. Jake, John Belushi's character, is resistant at first, but becomes mesmerized by the music. Then he has a spiritual experience.

A bright light from the heavens shines through an arch-shaped church window onto him, and Jake feels he hears a revelation from God. Jake is captivated by his epiphany, does backflips in the church aisle, and dances in front of the congregation. (The acrobatics of the rotund Jake are evidence that God *does* perform miracles!)

Once returning to Elwood, Jake tells him they *have* to get their band back together to play one last gig. It's how they can legitimately raise the cash for the orphanage. With a new purpose, the Blues Brothers approach their former bandmates. They are reluctant. Most are working in another band or at a restaurant. But Jake and Elwood are determined and persuasive.

They tell them, "We are on a mission from God!' Notwithstanding an argument with the Blues Brothers, or with God, the band reunites. Through wild car chases by the police and a country-western band, heavy combat attacks by Jake's ex-girlfriend, and obsessive vengeance by the Illinois Nazis (which my youngest daughter asked, "What are Yahtzees?"), they find a way to complete their mission.

I want to be like that...an artist on a mission from God!

I used to look at my life in a small Western town and employment at a nonprofit business and consider my creative gifts as supplemental and nonessential. My perspective was that my artistic gifts were like B-roll, secondary footage for a film which might be used or tossed away on the editing floor.

What's Your Mission?

In *The Heart of the Artist*, author Rory Noland contemplates the purpose of the artist and their role in society. And I had a vision. People were dancing in the aisles...no, that's Jake's vision! My mission from God started with the realization that artists are essential, not optional, to the human experience. Artists are not just the entertainment for the weekend. Artists interpret the long-running, day-by-day drama of mankind. And therefore, it's a sacred mission full of purpose.

For the next few months, I frequently replayed this new idea of the necessity of artists. At the time, I was a creative director who led and encouraged other artists. I witnessed many creative teammates become aware of their artistic talents. It seemed my mission included providing opportunities for artists to grow and develop. Yet, if I was an artist first and a leader second, shouldn't I have my own artistic mission?

Without a bright floodlight from Heaven as Jake had, I searched for my mission. I decided to say yes to any artistic opportunity that came my way. I took a pastel chalk class and saw tonal differences in color by squinting my eyes. I took a Bob Ross painting seminar and drew happy trees. Then a writing opportunity came about.

As usual, our group of artists was planning and preparing for the Christmas eve services.

We had an idea for a short ten-minute drama, but the regular writers were busy and didn't have the time to pen out the sketch. I was passionate about the idea and strongly felt the drama would enhance the church service, so I volunteered to write the short skit. Initially, I was thrilled to take on the writing adventure, but that gave way to fears of inadequacy. *Who was I to write a drama for an estimated audience of fifteen hundred people?* Then, crippling panic set in like a teenage girl in a slasher film running through a dark forest from hockey masked, ultra-villain Jason Voorhees. I couldn't scream aloud. No one ever hears the victims scream in a movie. Plus, it would have traumatized my children and prompted my team of artists to slip Prozac in my coffee.

Four days before the short drama script was due to be handed to the actors, I found my way out of the writing horrors and sat down with pen and paper and wrote. Scene by scene, I conceived of and developed the characters actions and dialogue. I spent a day editing and then emailed it to a few trusted colleagues for feedback. We made a few more adjustments and then I emailed it to the drama director with specific instructions that I didn't want anyone to know I was the author of the drama. The actors memorized the lines and rehearsed the stage blocking. Christmas Eve came and I, half fearful and half excited, watched the drama unfold. My panic eased as I saw the actors giving life to the written words, *my words*. My boss leaned over and said, "This is good, really good!"

After the service, I heard more compliments about the drama. Many people felt it was a realistic screenshot of adult children coming home for Christmas and their struggle with belief in the Nativity story they knew as kids. To each inquiry about the author of the sketch, we said one of our own artists had written it.

Was I feeling insecure about my writing skills? Definitely! Was I gutless about putting my name on the sketch? Oh yes! It was easier to take the risk by being incognito to the audience and actors. Plus, remaining anonymous allowed me to hear honest views of the drama. It gave me the opportunity to be part of the discussion without others compensating for my sensitivity and insecurity. It allowed me to hear unfiltered critiques and learn.

Taking on the writing assignment stretched my creative muscles. I didn't know if I could write a drama until I decided to try. This risk gave me a sense of confidence in my writing skills and the thrill of being on the dangerous side of an artistic venture. It was so amazing to sit off stage and watch the audience interact with the actors and the story. I *was* an artist on a mission from God! My writing talent was and is essential in the adventure of mankind.

Bright Beams and Revelations

Bright beams of sunlight in church windows are a given. A voice declaring our mission from God is not. Well, for most of us anyway.

I didn't hear a voice telling me my mission. But since I knew I was an artist, I decided to be open to various creative endeavors. It wasn't as much about the art itself, but rather moving forward creatively. It was about taking small steps and exploring creativity.

Being in motion first starts with the inner voice. I thought over and over about the artist's importance to mankind. That changed my behavior. I said yes to creative opportunities. Eventually a chance to write appeared and my inner voice talked me through the fear and gave me courage to be creative. And while I was thrilled with the results it was also the positive feedback from others that clinched the commitment to the mission of writing. If people hated the drama, or hated my writing, I would have contemplated my next steps. Was it the wrong audience? Was it my writing style? Do I suck at writing and need a class? Do I suck at writing and need to pursue another creative path?

Heeding feedback is crucial to anyone's success. I had asked for other's input before the drama was given to the actors and before it hit the stage. However, the feedback confirmed what I knew in my heart. I knew it was good. And that's not bragging but accepting my artistry and the hard work I put into it.

I wrote my first drama more than fifteen years ago. It was the genesis of many more purposeful art projects which I'll share later in the book. I still believe today, as much as I did then, that being on a mission from God requires the determination of and focus like the Blues Brothers.

@%&! (Explosions) Happen!

In *The Blues Brothers*, there are several comical subplots. One is the cat and mouse game between the brothers and the police. Elwood and Jake are riding in their junky police car, bickering about Elwood's inability to keep in touch with their former bandmates, when Elwood drives through a yellow light. A couple of policemen see the incident and pull them over. An officer walks up to the car and asks to see Elwood's license, insisting he ran a red light. (In Elwood's defense, yellow and red can possibly look the same, especially when wearing black sunglasses at night!) Back in their squad car, the officers discover that Elwood has a suspended driver's license and is to be arrested. The officers approach the car, telling Elwood to step out of the vehicle. It only takes a few seconds to decide what to do. Elwood starts the car and takes off with the police chasing them. Jake is distraught by Elwood's impulse to flee the cops. He complains that he's going to end up back in jail. Elwood snaps back, "They're not going to catch us. *We're* on a mission from God!"

Fleeing the police wasn't Elwood's brightest idea. Yet his bold action came from knowing and accepting his mission. When focused on your artistic mission, a certainty of risk will be involved.

From my observation, there are different levels of artistic thrill seekers. Some of us will spontaneously stomp on the accelerator, loving the quick speed and g-forces pushing against our being. We enthusiastically challenge the creative norms. We

28

accelerate toward new ideas and causes.

Yet, some of us have to be intentionally pushed and strapped onto the artistic excursion.

We scream, complain, and worry throughout the wild ride. But at the end of the ride, we're so glad we were thrown into the adventure. Creative risks are more difficult. We like calculated plans.

Whether you go willingly or hesitantly, getting on and staying on the artistic ride is what counts. That brave move can give a green light to a lifestyle of adventure and focus in the midst of obstacles.

Another subplot in the movie involves Jake's ex-girlfriend, played by Carrie Fisher, stalking the brothers and firing massive missiles at them. The brothers are constantly in the midst of an explosion. Each time, Jake and Elwood rise out of the rubble, shake off the dust from their near-death experience, and carry on. They don't seem to be rattled by the attacks, nor do they leave their mission to run after her. It's almost like they expect the attacks and refuse to be detoured. They remain focused on their mission of reuniting the band and raising money for the orphanage.

Often, as unsteady and erratic human artists, we can resist a commitment to our mission. We wonder if we have the passion and stamina required to endure our artistic crusade. While I had explored many art forms, it was writing that had always filled me with excitement. Wanting to focus on my passion for words, I decided to invest in my mission from God and went to my first writer's conference.

After sitting through the writer's conference, I grew excited by the speakers' helpful teachings. It motivated me to keep writing. Although I dreamt of being an author and completing a book, I was easily distracted. There were lots of explosions trying to deter the mission: my sweet angelic children transforming into obnoxious ogre-like teenagers—*KaBoom!* Changing jobs from creative director to serving customers as demanding as Illinois Nazis—

KaPOW! It was easy to let the challenges redirect my mission, altering my focus, weakening my devotion to my artistic mission. I was sitting at my fourth writer's conference and realized I didn't want to be one of *those* people: they dress like authors (they are so easy to spot—look for a 1960s sports coat with brown corduroy patches on the sleeves and wearing black round glasses), talk about writing, go to writer's conferences, and yet never complete a book.

I had to commit to my mission from God. That included dedicating time to write and making goals to complete a chapter. Pledging to this purpose meant intentionally reading books to move my writing forward. Joining a writer's group provided accountability and encouragement to finish the first draft of this book. Sure, life's challenges took me away from writing for a week or two. Sometimes for longer. But then I would put "write" on my calendar and make it happen. Even if it was for thirty minutes. I view my art like any other healthy habit. I floss. I eat greens. I write.

Should You Choose to Accept Your Mission

After a life of messing around and getting into trouble, the God-given mission issued Jake and Elwood Blues a new purpose and focus. The band enjoyed creating music together, but this time, the purpose of music was different. It went beyond their own love of music to include benefiting others. They wanted to help the orphanage stay in existence by providing money for the taxes. Whether it was gratitude to the nuns who raised them, or empathy for the orphans, their crusade affected others.

The Blues Brothers and their band used their art as an act of service. Their music gave the paying concert-goers a fun experience with a few cartwheels by Jake. They raised enough cash to pay the taxes, which allowed the orphans to have a home.

The Blues Brothers and their band choose to create for a

purpose larger than their self-interest.

This gave them focus and passion which affected many. In Chapter 9, we'll look at different artistic roles which can bring fulfillment and purpose to your creative dreams.

For most of my life, I have written for myself and my sanity. I have stacks of old journals under my bed chronicling the joys and sorrows, hopes and disappointments of my life. Journaling for fifteen to thirty minutes in the morning is as cleansing for my mind and soul like a hot shower is for the body. It's my method to work out the problems of the day and write out the prayers for tomorrow. Journaling helps me, but composing this book is my way to encourage and motivate others, and to have a purpose larger than myself.

If my artist's life were made into a movie, I wouldn't want it to resemble a two-hour documentary of defeat and meaningless wonderings. Rather, I want my life to be a series of moving pictures showing my devotion to my mission from God. I wish to be viewed as a heroine who persevered through the dry prairies and wilderness peaks of the artist's journey. I wouldn't want to be portrayed as a mere daredevil who took haphazard risks for the sake of personal glory or attention, but a determined woman who risked artistic complacency and inspired others to join the creative mission from God.

Should you choose to accept the mission, it's important to see it as a sacred path—an assignment to be cherished and protected. No matter how difficult it gets, we can't abandon the mission and succumb to the enemy of convenience, complacency, or selfishness. Fulfilling the mission means too much to us.

To creatively move yourself forward, reflect on the following questions.

Mission Statistics

1. What's your "Mission from God"? Do you need to search for it?
2. Have you committed yourself to your artist's journey? Why or why not?
3. On a scale of one to ten, where do you rate as an artistic risk-taker (one being not at all, ten being extreme)?
4. What explosions keep you from committing to your art?
5. Choose a current explosion or imagine a challenge which would keep you from creating. Write out a plan on how you would overcome it. Think about your self-talk, behavior, and emotions, and strategize how you will rise from the rubble.
6. Watch the movie *La La Land.* What was Sebastian's mission? What was Mia's mission? What were their explosions? What inspiration can you glean from Mia and Sebastian?
7. What new adventures do you anticipate as an artist?

A man either lives life as it happens to him, meets it head-on and licks it, or he turns his back on it and starts to wither away.
—Gene Roddenberry

Chapter 4
Entering the Alternate Universe

In an episode of *Star Trek* called "Mirror, Mirror," Captain Kirk and his team are on a planet to make a peaceful deal for supplies. As the crew is being "beamed" back to their ship, an ion storm in the atmosphere causes the transporter to malfunction. This glitch in the transporter system sends Kirk and crew members Scotty, Uhura, and McCoy to the starship Enterprise in a barbaric parallel universe. The people and the ship look the same, but the mission and customs contradict the team's normal world.

Captain Kirk and his crew soon realize they aren't in their home galaxy and attempt to adjust to the alternate universe. They pretend to play their expected roles of captain, engineer, communicator, and doctor, all the while adapting to the cultural nuances of the situation. The crew experiences confusion, misunderstanding, and distrust as they look for a way back to their home galaxy.

As an artist, I often feel like I'm living in an alternate universe.

It's where white walls and gray fabric cubicles are efficient and uninspiring. It's where a black Bic pen and the customary navy suit are rigid and boring. It's where the large, black three-ring binders of rules and procedures safeguard conformity and stifle novel ideas. If you have dedicated yourself to being an artist, you've probably been "beamed" there too.

In my home universe, my artistic nature enjoys creativity, playfulness, and originality. It's comfortable and normal. But in the galaxy of my work experience with the step-by-step procedures, strict schedules, and repetitive outcomes, my creative being endures discomfort and stress. Living in this corporate universe, I feel out of sync and out of place. Occasionally, I am misunderstood and judged. Frustration and disappointment with non-artists cause me to build protective walls or search for a way out of the foreign universe.

Of course, the crew of Star Trek has an advantage. They know they've landed in a quirky rendition of the Federation galaxies. (TV reality gives about forty-two minutes to figure it out.) For me though, the realization has been slow, like watching pixels render grid by grid to form an image. The first indication I might be dealing with an alien group of people in another galaxy happened when I attended a private college.

Nonconformist or Rebel?

Marcie, a typical alien, blinked her large blue eyes twice and leaned forward. "Are you a rebel or just a nonconformist?"

What? Confused by her question, my first response was to laugh at the incredulous idea that I was different. "What do you mean?"

We sat on the serrated steel stairs outside the dorm we both lived in, enjoying the humid spring day in Missouri. Marcie wrung her slender hands. "You painted random cinder blocks in your room purple. Most people would have painted the whole wall. Your desk and bed are placed at angles and pictures dangle from the ceiling. And the way you dress is nontraditional, a little too flamboyant. Plus you disregard the rules." She concluded, "It's just not…" Marcy lifted her slim ivory fingers and used the dreaded air quotes, "'normal.'"

I defended my offbeat style. "I don't consider myself a rebel and I don't try to be a nonconformist." *And what is 'normal'?*

The stimulating conversation jolted me into introspection and analysis of my behavior and motives. It was frustrating to be misunderstood. I thought others viewed the world as I did— white cinder block walls need to be painted. I didn't realize that my clothes communicated something other than colorful and fun.

When I landed in the workplace, one of the first things I did was purchase a gallon of paint and start dressing those naked white walls. As a creative director for a nonprofit organization, I had a vision of what I wanted my office to look and feel like. I chose a pale yellow base coat paint with a deeper sunflower yellow glaze to give warm texture to the north-facing dark room. I purchased a print of Michelangelo's *The Creation* to hang on the yellow wall as creative inspiration. I added a soothing water feature, glowing scented candles, and a red bubble gum dispenser machine to create a positive ambience. Apparently, this had never happened in the office building before!

After walking in my office, people would ask why I painted the walls yellow. The janitors nervously calculated the number of coats of alabaster paint it would take to cover my happy yellow walls! (Fifteen years later, I bumped into a person who stated with a chuckle, "Yes, I remember those egg yolk yellow walls.") Especially men made comments about the naked Adam, painted by Michelangelo. Some casually asked, "Shouldn't you have office art like the teamwork picture of skydivers in here?" Others, thinking I was oblivious or blind, asked, "Did you realize that there is a picture of a naked man in your office?"

I wasn't intentionally rebelling against the office norms. Honestly! I merely tried to create a place where artists wanted to hang out. I wanted to both inspire others and be inspired by my office space. I was slow in recognizing how my creative disposition often put me in opposition to corporate cultural norms and rules.

When faced with a challenging situation, I use my imagination to call forth a variety of ideas and possibilities. My artistic drive to be original allows me to look at work-related issues from different angles. This often results in challenging routines, defying the status quo, and sometimes, breaking the rules. You see, my quest for creativity and originality often guides me with a different set of norms and rules.

The challenge we face as artists living in the alternate universe workplace is that most businesses love conformists. A person who comfortably lives inside the box of policies and facts is a highly desirable employee. Granted, an organization needs to align people for the purpose of their mission. Rules and regulations give employees and organizations structure.

The successful company operates on data and numbers. And many Spock-like people thrive in the world of statistics, ratios, and quotas. A good company man or woman doesn't ask too many questions, or challenge the current conditions, and thinks nothing of the white walls. They are good, stable, hardworking people. And for much of my life I tried desperately to blend in and be like them.

At times, I squelch ideas or thoughts about work-related situations to avoid chastisement. I go along with the situation to avoid disrupting the continuum of the mirror galaxy. I suppress my artistic nature for fear of receiving stinging criticism. This eventually results in creative outbursts and playful rebellion, which is met with a confused stare and raised eyebrow that ask, "What planet are you from?"

On Halloween, everyone at work dressed up according to the theme each department chose. I emailed a friend describing my costume and work situation: *Our team decided to dress as golfers. In years past we've been different comic characters such as Batman and Robin. We've also dressed as circus entertainers such as trapeze artists, clowns, and lion-tamers. We were all in for our costumes and themes.*

I continue typing fast and furious: *But this year, my coworkers wanted to be comfortable on the most likely very busy Halloween Friday. We voted on the golfer idea and it won. I'm not excited about the idea. It seems so uncreative and unoriginal. But I decided to be a tree at the golf course. You know, the tree which endures abuse from beginner or frustrated golfers, and in turn steals their golf balls, tees, and maybe even an ill-thrown iron. My golf course tree is rather creative though I doubt any of my golfer coworkers notice or appreciate it!* And I hit SEND.

With this grand vision of a tree on the golf course in mind, I found a brown church monk's costume for the tree trunk. Then I bought some glittery green netting and cut it to look like flowing tree leaves. I had found some Christmas golf ball ornaments (now I understand why stores have Christmas merchandise out before Halloween) and hung those on the netting "leaves." I hot-glued golf tees, golf balls, and leaves to a red wig. I put on the outfit and looked in a rectangle standing mirror. I was a life-sized piece of mixed-media art!

My coworkers asked why I wasn't wearing knickers and made comments that it wasn't what we agreed on as a group. I acknowledged that I went AWOL with my costume. Then I explained my thought process about the golf course tree. Some raised their eyebrows as if they instinctively knew I wasn't from their planet, but many of my peers laughed and embraced my creative individualism. Soon the executives and the costume judges came by for a look at my Halloween attire.

"We heard about your costume and had to take a look," declared one leader.

Another boss asked with a wink, "Do you have my five iron in your branches?"

By noon, the costume judging team made the decision for best Halloween costume and handed out the fifty-dollar gift card prize, and it wasn't given to any of the golfers. No, the golf course tree won and took home the green!

My winning Halloween costume was a victory for creativity over conformity, and a triumph for originality over status quo. It's good to conform to social etiquette. It's smart to conform to job protocols. And it's wise to follow moral codes. *But* there are situations where rebels or nonconformists are needed within the gray cubicle walls.

Do you know what happened after I painted my walls sunshine yellow? Artists came into my office and lingered there, chatting about creative ideas and hopes. Other coworkers painted one wall blue (okay, let's not get too rebellious!) or added wainscoting panels to their offices. It was like the building came alive with the expressions of the people who worked in it. Individual creativity at the office became the accepted norm.

Do you know what happened after the Halloween golf tree won? The staff pushed for original ideas for branch contests to build positive teamwork. In the midst of office tension or tediousness, creativity was a source of lightheartedness and liveliness. You see, a touch of creativity ignites the spirit of those around you. A spark of originality pushes others to also think outside the gray box. The aliens want to be creative too. They don't always know it, but they need a flash of nonconformity in their lives to awaken the new and innovative. As the new business model becomes tradition, a rebel or nonconformist is needed to go above "the way we've always done it" to "it seems unorthodox but let's try it."

Listening to my innovative gut bolstered the courage and confidence I needed to be an artist piloting through the alien universe. I intentionally steered through the typical negativity of those who love conformity. Even though I thoroughly enjoyed the hole-in-one experience, I still had a lot to learn about communication in the alternate universe.

Learning the Alien Language

Every month, I wrote a report to the board of the organization where I worked. I highlighted various achievements and challenges in my worship arts department. Usually my reports glowed with magical Leprechauns dancing by pots-of-gold-at-the-end-of-rainbow scenarios as I recapped all the great things the artists were creating. But one month, I couldn't escape the reality that the Leprechauns had lost energy amid the mostly dry conditions of the organization. Wanting to keep it real, I decided to communicate the effects that the organizational budget cuts had on my department. I wrote, "Because of the lack of funds, I'm not able to take the artists on our annual retreat and arts conference. This lack of creative rest and input negatively affects the team members. The artists are experiencing a creative exhaustion and burnout."

Soon I received a call from my supervisor informing me that my report had upset the board chairman. I couldn't understand how telling the truth about the artists' struggles was offensive. I decided to call the chairman and talk to him.

Tightly gripping my cell phone and keeping my voice level, I asked him, "I heard my report caused some concern on your part. Can you explain to me what made you upset?"

I heard quiet breathing through my phone. Then a deliberate, gravelly voice said, "I'm confused about the term creative exhaustion. The volunteer musicians and drama people have a job to do and they need to quit whining. And if they are tired, maybe they're not necessary."

After a discussion in which I asked questions, clarified terms, and listened to the chairman's perspective, I realized I had been using the wrong language. Remembering he was a businessman with a farm, I asked him, "What would happen if year after year you planted corn in the same field?"

"The plant would struggle to grow and produce ears of

corn," he answered.

"What would happen if you didn't rest that field or planted a crop that replenished the nutrients in the soil?"

"We wouldn't have a crop."

"What would happen if you hooked a milk cow up to a milking machine for twenty-four hours a day? Got milk?"

I heard fumbling sounds over the phone connection like he had moved his phone from one hand to the other, and then a long sigh.

"Okay, I think I see what you were referring to in your report," he conceded.

Using familiar language and terms with the board chairman cleared the way to effective communication. I first had to understand his mindset to effectively communicate and be heard.

Not only do the aliens perceive the world differently, I realized that they speak different dialects. In dealing with the alternate universe, I've learned to adapt my communication to my audience.

As with the logical Spock, speech such as "the creative concept isn't coming to me, so I haven't started the art project," does not connect with the alien people. Because they don't create art, they may not understand the time and energy necessary to envision and complete a piece of art. They may not understand the imagination's need for rest and creative stimulus. They may lack respect for the creative work that involves the mind, heart, and soul of the artist.

When conversing about art or artists with the aliens, it's best to be concise and clear. Tell them about the vision and logistics. Talk in terms of time frame, estimated budget, and bottom line. For instance, "We are planning an art show for elementary aged children around the theme of beginnings. It will run for the month of June and families will enjoy seeing their child's work in the gallery." Their eyes may glaze over if we talk about mixed media, collage, or watercolors. The aliens live mostly in their minds. If we delve too deeply into artist jargon, it will only confuse and disengage them in the conversation. That being said, every connection with the aliens is an opportunity to influence, educate, and persuade. It's a chance to dissolve stereotypes and misunderstandings of artists which cause division or result in taking sides in the alternate universe.

Breaking Through Barriers

As in the mirror world where Captain Kirk survives an assassination attempt and warns his team to watch their backs, I once fostered distrust and dislike for the aliens. For many years, I regret to admit, I succumbed to an "us versus them" attitude. "Us" referred to the artists who were passionate about their creative expression through the arts. "Them" referred to those who dared to "not get it" or criticized the art form. The wall between "us' and "them" was formidable as the Great Wall of China. For many years, I loved the wall. It protected me and "us." We artists enjoyed the safety of our community. Within our boundaries we created and shared our works of art with each other. We discussed our techniques and encouraged innovative risk. While we created and shared within the group, it soon became apparent that the walls that protected "us" also restricted our influence on "them."

The artist team decided to have our first art show. I eagerly chose a few of my best photographs and had them matted and framed. Excited to share their creativity, the artists brought their mixed media and watercolor, acrylic, and oil paintings along with photography to exhibit.

During the art show, I watched and talked to people as they experienced the art. A man approached me and told me how he admired my image of the sunset over the ocean. He stated that he enjoyed the rich purple and pink colors of the sun and its reflection over the ocean. He especially loved how I was able to capture the bubbles from the outgoing tide on the sand. It reminded him of growing up in Puerto Rico and the happy memories of playing in the ocean. As we were finishing our conversation, the board chairman came up to me.

He pointed to a canvas depicting a close-up of Jesus's eyes, one swollen shut and the other open and looking straight at you as He hung on the cross. It was done in rich hues of blue and crimson oil paint by one of my artist friends. It was unique in appearance and full of emotional tension.

He softly confided, "I've read the Easter story many times in my seventy years of living, but I've never seen such a vivid picture of suffering."

The man, who at one time thought us artists as whiny and unnecessary, was now emotional over a portrait of the bruised face of Jesus. "This portrait has given me a new picture of the old story of Easter. Thank you for putting on the art show." He shook my hand and turned to leave.

As I watched the large elderly man hobble toward the door, it became apparent to me that my art, my passion and desire to creatively communicate, was truly for "them."

Yes, generating art enlarges my soul and gives me a sense of fulfillment. It's safe and enjoyable to participate in artistic communities. But when the wall between "us" and "them" is torn down by sharing our art, the aliens in the alternate universe awaken to their unrealized emotions and alter their thinking. Art is the portal to a new thought, concept, or action. It can challenge a person to reframe their personal way of living. Art is like the mirror that captures the image of their emotions and intellect and reflects it back to them. Until they see that reflection, they may not have been aware those emotions existed.

Breaking down the barriers between "us" and "them" creates a flow of influence with our art. While not all aliens will understand our creativity, our challenge is to knock out a brick in the wall and improve the communication of our artistry.

It Takes a Personal Revolution

At the conclusion of the "Mirror, Mirror" episode, the misplaced Star Trek team is about to be "beamed" back to the Enterprise in their home galaxy. Captain Kirk gives a passionate challenge to the bearded alternate Spock: "In every revolution, there is a man with a vision."

Kirk challenges Spock's logic of accepting the current status in the alternate universe. He asks Spock to find a plausible reason to choose freedom over tyranny, the future over the past. Spock, who has been positively influenced by the Kirk of another galaxy, tells him that he will consider it. And then Spock enables the transporter, sending Captain Kirk and his team back to their home universe.

I've wasted my energies fretting over the unsuitable, artist-starved atmosphere of the alternate universe. I've spent too much time looking for an escape from the aliens. Instead, I should have sought a vision for my artist journey within the un-creative galaxy. With memories of the changed board chairman as he looked at the oil painting and the surprised pleasure of the executives as they looked at my golf course tree costume, I realize the impact art can have on a person and community.

It's these experiences which prompt the need for an artist's vision. I want to reach my fullest potential as an artist *and* fulfill a need in the uncreative lives of the aliens. I'm no longer *just* devoted to being an artist for myself and other artists. As I witness how art helps those in the alternate universe to process their life, I realize the power of art to translate across the wormhole divide. And if you are going to bravely fly through a wormhole, a flight plan, a personal artist's vision, is necessary.

First, I went into brainstorm mode and asked myself, "What core values do I embrace and use as guiding lights for my vision?" (You can find a list of core values on Pinterest or Google.) The activity directed me to circle twenty values, and then whittle the twenty down to nine, and eventually three core values. I sat on my bed staring at the twenty words. *Do I cross out humility or adventure? Should I keep creativity or resilience?* I stared a little longer. Suddenly I saw how all twenty fit into my top three values.

My core values are health, creativity, and humility.

I want to have a healthy mind, healthy emotions, and a healthy body. The wellness of my mind and emotions positively affect my relationships with family, friends, fellow artists, and the checkout clerk at Walmart. (I'll discuss more about emotions in the next chapter.) The fitness of body and mind requires healthy nutrition and exercise. It includes humor and fun. It speaks to the balance of work and play, alone time and quality relationships. Unhealthiness in any of those areas robs me of joy and imagination. It also prevents me from leading my best life possible isn't that what we all want?

I value creativity because it is who I am and what I strive to bring to others. The beauty and uniqueness of creativity inspires me, and I yearn to share this with others. Creativity is intentional and purposeful. I don't know about you, but whether it's taking a picture with my iPhone, planting a rose, or writing a story, it's all done with motive and meaning. Creativity can have an element of playfulness which brings enjoyment. To live in an uncreative, unbeautiful place is like death to me, stripping away energy and enthusiasm.

Humility is my response to all of life. I know...it's an unusual one. I'll go deeper into humility in the next chapter, but it's not a natural response for me. As with most humans, I naturally feel I'm not enough—I should be *more* artistic, *more* intelligent, *more* appreciated, etc., and I strive to prove my worth. Claiming humility as a core value requires personal transparency and authenticity because I own a proper view of self. I don't have to act more important than you because we are both important. I can applaud your accomplishments because my worth isn't diminished by your achievements. Humility requires a depth of soul which is stronger than seeking popularity and self-promotion. Humility enhances creativity by seeking to learn from others. Driven by pride and ego only hurts my relationships and diminishes authentic creativity.

Discovering your core values may take time. If you are struggling to pinpoint your values, put the list away for a while. Take a shower, go for a walk, and come back to the list. I guarantee you will get down to your three basic core values.

This internal exercise of defining core values is important as a navigation tool to setting up goals, activities, and relationships. Values guide me to which goal I should pursue, and why I should say no to certain activities or people. My vision doesn't just dictate my goals and to-do lists but guides me in determining my character and reputation. A personal vision is about creating a legacy before it happens.

The next step is to write a vision statement. It can be as short as a sentence or as long as a page. It doesn't have to be perfect. In fact, you will periodically refine and polish your vision throughout the year. But it needs to describe who you want to become. While most motivational gurus will advise to write your vision, you can also get creative. I'm a visual learner, so I opted to create a vision board.

I bought a cork board, found quotes and pictures, and made a collage of my artistic vision. I have it hanging where I can see it every morning when I dress for work in the alternate universe, and every evening when I pull on my leggings and sweatshirt. It makes me smile when I look at it. I feel courage when I read the quotes. I am focused on the future when I look at the various pictures. It transforms my mind and heart. And soon my actions will follow my mind and heart. And this is where the revolution begins.

A few episodes after the Star Trek "Mirror, Mirror" episode, it's revealed that the Spock in the alternate universe becomes captain of the starship Enterprise. He leads a rebellion against the evil Federation and defends the freedom of other alien groups. Though Kirk was displaced from his home universe, his unorthodox behavior influenced Spock and changed the alternate galaxy.

Are you a rebel or nonconformist? I'm probably both. As an explorer of creativity and humanity, I must go beyond the boundaries normally held in the alternate universe. It is my inquisitive and unbridled nature which shakes up the conformity and sparks new perspectives. My imaginative and risk-taking style is exactly what the art-starved lives of the alien people crave. Anything less, or different, *would not* or *could not* accomplish the purpose I was created for.

Pursuing my artistic vision feels like a nosedive into the wormhole. It is an ear-popping, heart-pumping, mind-blowing g-force of grit and potential. Without the details and calculation of my vision, I miss the wormhole, the relationships with the aliens, and the artist's revolution never begins. The alternate universe will carry on without my creative intervention. It will continue to conform to the predictable and exist in the status quo.

Therefore, "us" artists are to be the nonconformists who jar the aliens from their common rut of routine to experience fascinating anomalies. We are the mavericks who elevate the human soul out of the status quo to a level of personal transcendence. We must start an artist's revolution which frees the aliens from their inner captivities. And we must meet them in their daily, white wall, gray cubicle world.

It's time to plan your artist's vision. It's time to jot down the necessary values and goals. It's time to use the questions below to ignite your personal revolution.

Flight Plan

1. What are the challenges of being an artist in your workplace, family or community?
2. What does "being a brave artist" mean to you?
3. What actions reflect artistic bravery?
4. How can you begin your own artist's revolution?

5. Take a weekend to identify your core values and artistic mission. Write your vision and post it where you can read it daily. Or create a vision board, using quotes and pictures, to motivate you toward growing as an artist.

6. TV shows like *Mash*, *Cheers*, *Seinfeld*, and *Friends* had the highest viewership for the show's finale. Watch one of the final episodes and write about how it made you feel. Were you sad to see it end? Why did society like the characters? How has our culture changed because of that TV show?

I am thankful for the opportunity to express the emotions of life through the art of dance.
—Rhee Gold

Chapter 5
Balance in the Wings

A silhouette of a woman waits behind a red curtain. She carefully rehearses her dance steps while conscious of the low murmurs and occasional giggles of people taking their seats on the other side of the curtain. She takes deep breaths to slow her excited heart and refocuses on the movements of her hands and feet.

The strums of the guitar begin, and the woman slowly steps out of the wings into the sprays of overhead lights in a huge French Rococo-styled ballroom. A male dancer walks toward the woman from the other side of the room. He gives her an affectionate embrace and they gently move side to side in rhythm to the soft guitar music. The woman, in a white bustier and mid-length mesh white skirt, twists away only to have the man pull her back to his arms. And they again sway in unison. Clothed in a black vest and pants, he lifts her, cradling her horizontal to the ground. They whirl around the floor until he safely sets her down, and they continue their intimate dance. During the dance routine, while the couple sits on the wood floor, the man lifts the woman's leg and playfully strums her calf as if he's playing his guitar. With hints of modern ballroom steps, lifts, and catches, the man gracefully leads the woman through the passionate highs and lows of their romance. I tap the play arrow on the computer and watch the artistry again.

Even with the music muted, the details of the dancers touching hands, their syncopated steps, and the wistful gaze of their eyes overwhelm me. My throat constricts and my eyes water. I envy the gorgeous long-haired brunette as I fall a teeny bit in love with the ginger-haired male dancer.

It's one of the most exquisite pieces of art I've ever encountered. And as beauty often does, it causes me to be crazy and obsessed. I develop a callous on the tip of my finger from repeatedly hitting the play arrow. My eyes are red from the strain of staring at my computer screen. And not only that, but the dance was an emotional workout for my soul.

Emotion: the awful, beautiful, confusing, electric, and intense state of mind and heart which has plagued me since I was young. "Don't be so sensitive," I heard from family.

"Are you going to cry?" I heard from friends.

Emotion is both my friend and my antagonist. It lifts my confidence to write with depth and vulnerability, and it accuses me of inept and ignorant writing skills. Emotion causes me to be a warrior battling for my artistic vision. And it also prompts me, many times, to cower from the criticisms of others. My emotions hoist me to extreme joys, and my moods plummet to despondent depression. Emotion whirls and twirls me around life's ballroom, leaving me, at times, dizzy and winded.

Others say artists are moody; we say we're emotional and feel deeply. Coworkers perceive us as difficult, but we say we're passionate about our vision. A boss tells us we are insecure and can't handle criticism. We say we're vulnerable when we create something with our heart only to have others judge it. While others see a white flower, we notice an English rose with thirty petals in shades of white and gray and overtones of pink. And that may make us perfectionists—or careful observers.

As artists, *we are* moody, deep, difficult, visionary, insecure, sensitive, and passionate.

And there's a scientific reason. Research by Elaine N. Aron, PhD, in her book *The Highly Sensitive Person: How to Thrive When the World Overwhelms You* (2013), shows that twenty percent of the worldwide population are highly sensitive people (HSP). And since traits of HSP are often found in creative people, Aron predicts the percentage is higher among artists. Aron describes HSP traits as: exhibiting a sensitive nervous system, an awareness of subtleties in his/her surroundings, and being easily overwhelmed by a highly stimulating environment (2013).

Like HSPs, artists tend to have an exceptional depth of emotion not found in non-artists. It's like carrying around a five-gallon bucket of emotions versus the lighter teacup others hold. Similar to HSPs, we are acutely aware of everything happening around us. The sensory overload of social media, constant global news, and the hurried gait of life generates a demanding need for us perceptive types to withdraw and spend time in solitude. And since we sense inner and outer emotions more strongly, our physiology is also more responsive to medications, caffeine, and stress. Being an artist and HSP mimics the partnership of a dance couple who strive for harmony in their steps and the beat of the music.

The Duet Dance of Artist and Emotions

"I am highly sensitive and emotional," my friend Leah Beauchamp confesses as she takes another drink of her frappe. We're in a vintage cafe, a renovated 1900s theater brimming with the earthy aroma of coffee, to discuss her artistic journey.

"So am I!" I blurt out my secret and Leah's eyes widen a bit at the revelation. My voice trembles as I relate the struggle of being a covert highly sensitive person. "I've learned to hide my emotions, because I grew up believing they were weak or wrong."

My mind jumps to a time in my early teens when my grandmother bluntly told me I was getting fat. I cringed from embarrassment and hurt. I didn't eat for a month and felt depressed for two months. My family couldn't understand why Grandma's criticism hurt me so much and I couldn't quickly forget about it. After all, she wasn't exactly skinny-minny, my family reminded me. I overheard my mom and sisters talking about me, stating that if they ignored my sadness, I would eventually get over it. It was one of the many times I tried to communicate my emotions to friends and family, and they didn't comprehend or validate my tender emotions.

I wasn't just sensitive to others' criticism, but also to scary or sad movies. The unsettling emotions from the story plots lingered with me for days. On top of that, it's difficult for me to visit people in the hospital because I vicariously feel their pain. One time, a woman lifted her hospital gown to show the large metal staples holding her gut together. When I saw the pus- seeping, rosy-red incision, I physically felt a jab of pain like a knife cutting open my torso. I emotionally experienced her frustration toward her confinement to a hospital bed. Because of this, I don't watch doctor or slasher shows either!

I didn't realize that I exhibited traits of a highly sensitive person. I always knew I had tender emotions, but I didn't understand it. Usually, I covered my emotional depth with a calm level-headed exterior. Not so for Leah.

"Being highly sensitive has caused turmoil in my relationships with family and friends, especially with non-artists," Leah somberly explains. "When I try to share how I feel some say, 'Oh, that's so nice.' I can tell they don't get me." This, she says, causes severe misunderstandings with others.

Nevertheless, her goal as an artist is to be authentic, raw, honest, and generous with what is inside of her. Whether in a reaction to relationships or in playing a part in a show, Leah has vowed to be completely herself. As I listen to Leah acknowledge and accept her sensitivity, I admire her gentle confidence that becomes strength.

Leah looks every bit the dancer in black capris, a long sleeve shirt, and a mint green puffer vest as she expresses how important emotions are to dancing. "Dance is intellectual but very intimate when expressing through art." Leah continues, "As dancers learn the choreography, they're in each other's physical space and also share emotional space. This leads to the necessity of building trust among the dance partnership or group."

Earlier this year, Leah was rehearsing to play the spring fairy when she suffered a miscarriage of her second baby. As she grieved her loss, Leah found it difficult to play the ditzy, happy fairy the role demanded. Through her emotionally turbulent time, the dance family encircled Leah with support and encouragement. Her next dance role required Leah to thrash her body on the floor, pounding the hardwood with her fists. By physically pouring her grief into her character, she was able to emotionally heal from her miscarriage.

With a sigh of satisfaction Leah reiterates, "Being sensitive can feel like a detriment at times, but if properly channeled, can improve my art." And that's exactly what Leah's emotional struggle accomplished. Following her performances, an attendee told Leah, "I love to watch you dance. It touches my soul."

As artists, it's crucial we learn healthy responses to our emotions. Often, we have unhealthy reactions such as faking, hiding, drugging, numbing, babying, or flinging them at others. Our goal is to unify our emotions to dance with our logic. Emotions, on their own, can pull us to illusions of self-grandeur. Our moods can push us to insurmountable walls of depression. They lie to us, demand power over us, minimize the importance of our rationale. Emotions can cause us to make mistaken judgments of others and misuse emotions. exposing us as stumbling, uncoordinated buffoons. I witnessed a situation where mismanaged emotions of a leader was not only embarrassing, they also caused distrust in relationships.

The band was busy setting up amps and connecting cords, as

the vocalists ruffled through the music and played with their microphones. When all the cords had been plugged into the sound system, the instrumentalists strummed their guitars or plucked the piano keys for a sound check. As usual, there was silence from one of the guitars. And the investigation began to find which cord had the evil gremlin blocking the guitar from being heard over the sound system. There was unplugging of cords, re-plugging of new cords, and the pushing of buttons on the sound board. The band leader, who was also the lead vocalist, stood on stage and yelled out to the sound tech, "Are you completely inept?"

He jumped off the stage, ran up to sound board, and leaned in front of the sound tech and started pushing buttons. I could hear the tech defensively saying, "I tried that. I checked that. That's not the problem."

The band leader ran back onto the stage and told the guitarist to play again. We all looked at the silent black speakers. Frustrated and angry, the band leader started kicking the amps and music stands and stomped off the stage.

"Oh great. Not again," said a vocalist.

"Glad he didn't yell at me," stated the drummer.

"Typical musician," commented the sound tech.

"Who's going to go get him?" asked the keyboard player.

"Play your guitar again," commanded the sound tech.

The guitarist again strummed his instrument and music flowed from the black speakers.

"Okay, someone has to go get him," pleaded the bass player.

"Not me!"

"Not me!"

"Forget him, let's run through the first song." The keyboard player looked at the drummer who lifted his drumsticks and clicked out the tempo.

Artists' behaving badly is self-sabotage. Yes, it's frustrating dealing with people! I understand that not everyone cooperates like a good dance partner. If you mingle with others, eventually you will get bruised and hurt in the dance of life. And the natural reaction to being hurt is to lash out at others. But when our emotions erupt and we behave badly, people look at *us* and not our creativity. Our appalling actions overshadow our art. Our negative behavior will deter opportunities. Oh, some will put up with our poor conduct, but when our emotions lead us, we resemble a two-year-old in a tutu tripping over our own feelings. It's through self-awareness that our emotions can "grow-up" and serve us well in both our art and life.

Self-Awareness as Our Healthy Partner

Leah introduced me to her sometimes dance partner Jonathan after I witnessed their performance at an outdoor venue. Their graceful ballet steps interpreted the raw emotions of rock music. The contrast made the dance dynamic and unforgettable.

Jonathan Hedger, in casual work clothes, drinks his orange juice as we chat at the same 1900s old theater-turned-coffee house where I met Leah. "All I want to do is pursue what I enjoy. It's hard for me to understand how people judge."

Jonathan tells me his story of how a friend asked him to join a dance class. Although he played baseball and enjoyed karate, Jonathan loved the music and the physical challenge of dance. And being one of the few boys in dance class had its perks too. The dance instructors and his female counterparts appreciated and adored Jonathan. But the positive emotions ended in the dance studio.

Jonathan found it challenging to be authentic about his passion for dance in the cowboy culture of Wyoming. Jonathan and his military family moved to Cheyenne when he was in fifth grade. By the time Jonathan was in junior high school, any mention of his interest in dance prompted ridicule from his peers. They accused him of being gay, and although Jonathan argued with them, they stereotyped his sexuality.

Jonathan's crystal blue eyes darken as he summarizes, "During my teen years, I tried to develop an emotionally tough skin and only talked to people at the dance studio."

Instead of allowing his emotions to become calloused, bitter, or repressed, Jonathan pursued a college degree in psychology to further understand his emotions. Jonathan worked on his self-image and wrestled with his bouts with depression. Through his studies, Jonathan learned the art of critical thinking. Rather than relying on his emotions to determine his perspective on the world, he analyzed and evaluated information using his intellect in decision-making. This self-awareness created personal growth in Jonathan bringing a healthier self to his art.

Jonathan believes carrying unresolved emotional issues onto the dance floor negatively influences his dance roles. It causes him to misinterpret or overplay his character's mood. An imbalanced emotional state also alters his relationships with his teachers, peers, and close friends within the dance studio where trust and collaboration are necessary. His emotional growth and acceptance of his highly sensitive nature allows him to care less what others think of his dance obsession, on most days.

Jonathan sets his empty bottle of Tropicana juice on the small white table between us.

"It's a daily task to balance my emotions."

Understanding the origins of our emotions is the first step in guiding them. To wait in the wings, out of sight of others, and assess our feelings, allows us to pinpoint issues needing extra focus. A time to reflect, figure out our sensitivities, and respond to our environment in healthy ways can untangle emotions.

A few years ago, Leah and her husband decided to leave her dancing career in Denver, Colorado, to return to Wyoming. At five months pregnant, she knew it was the right decision. Yet Leah understood Wyoming was not a place where dance was alive. Heartbroken, she felt her dance life was finished.

Leah gave birth to beautiful baby Brittany in May. The following September, Leah taught a few classes at the dance studio where she learned to dance. It wasn't the dreamy experience Leah expected. She resented the students in her class. They were young. They were free to dance. She had a baby. She wasn't free to dance. She envied her students. And guilt was added to her envious emotions.

During this time, a dance instructor came to Cheyenne and opened Ballet Wyoming Dance Company. As a former instructor, she remembered Leah's dance ability, and asked her to dance in the company's first show. Stretching her ballet legs and donning her dance shoes, Leah's body and soul danced again.

Reconnecting with dance had a significant effect on Leah. She noticed a change in her attitude toward her students and her life in Wyoming. Leah realized she taught dance in attempt to meet her needs, to get closer to the art she was longing for, and not for the benefits of the kids. Resuming her own dance routine allowed Leah to teach out of a healthier mind and heart. Instead of continuing in jealousy, Leah evaluated the root cause of her emotions and adjusted her behavior. This moved Leah forward to a better place with her students, herself, and her art.

Humble Steps

As Jonathan and I walk out of the coffee house, he emphatically tells me, "I desire humility not only for myself, but I aspire for others and for Ballet Wyoming to cultivate humility."

I'm intrigued. I seldom encounter a person who deliberately seeks humbleness. In fact, most people I know are concerned with the exact opposite. Most of us are consumed with promoting ourselves at work, fearful that we will be overlooked. I've become acquainted with the human need for humility through teachings at church, and most recently from my master's studies on servant leadership.

True humility is a balanced perspective recognizing one's strengths and weaknesses, and is open to the value of others' needs and perspectives. A humble person is confident but unassuming, always accountable to others. Humility is countercultural, counter-intuitive, and would seem counterproductive in the art business. For Jonathan, it's the footprint of his life.

"Being arrogant or prideful is a pitfall," Jonathan explains. "No one wants to work with you." Whether at work or in the dance studio, Jonathan choreographs his life with respect for others. This perspective is more of a student, rather than a dancer who has mastered all the steps and needs no further coaching or advice.

"I try not to overstate myself in any situation," Jonathan reveals. "There is always a desire to be the center of attention. I have found, however, that simply keeping your word and being attentive to your duties brings you far more than attempting to call attention to yourself in any other way."

The most difficult aspect of humbleness for Jonathan occurs when others admire his dance skills and look to learn from him. When others compliment him, Jonathan could proclaim himself the best dancer. Instead, Jonathan recognizes that he is the most experienced male dancer in the ballet company, but still has more dances to learn and accomplish. When Jonathan's dance students idolize him, his ego could soak up the adoration and become arrogant. Jonathan believes his responsibility is to instruct them, without belittling them, so they can understand the different aspects of dance. For Jonathan, humility happens in the small choices, the private, honest moments. "I believe it's those little things that cause the most impact overall, because they occur most often."

If we rush by the small moments, we miss opportunities to choose the best and deepest emotions. In our hurry, we ignore patience, love, or humility. When our reality becomes busy and overwhelming, we dangle in a vertigo state of mind, where nothing makes sense, and our mind becomes dizzy, unclear, and lacking self-awareness, allowing tipsy steps of pride, jealousy, insecurity, and even depression to rule our behavior. A step back from the frenzied pace helps us regain our emotional balance and sure footing. Pulling back from the hectic calendar and the pressure to create is necessary for the artist.

Feel Your Rhythm

Most people consider me a warm and friendly person. But there are days when I have no sparkle in my step. I'm overwhelmed by the demands of homework, work, relationships, and the general chaos of life. I'm anxious, cranky, and super-duper sensitive. It's like my sensory input jammed and I have to remove myself to reset my emotions.

As a teenager, I often walked on the dusty gravel roads, claiming peace from the clouds that drifted across the western sky. When I was in college, I escaped from the noisy populated dorm to a professor's empty house. There I turned on mellow music, dimmed the lights, and laid on the couch, insulating myself from the buzzing world. As an adult with children, I had less freedom to have my necessary retreat. Usually, I played the piano when the kids napped or walked in the park as a friend babysat. Now that the kids have left the household, I enjoy more flexibility in my schedule. My runs through the park give me the solitude I crave. I also engage in community Art Walks which expose me to a variety of creativity. After a few hours of quietness or creative stimulation, the emotional edginess dissipates, and I emerge back into society rejuvenated. When solitude doesn't refresh our creative energy or reset our emotions, our negative moods may indicate something deeper is out of step.

When attempting to understand our emotions, we must look at our family imprint. Our problem-solving skills came from following in the footsteps of the adults in our life. Our reactions to anger, conflict, joy, laughter, and affection have been choreographed by our parents, grandparents, or any influential caregiver. As we become adults, some of those generational traits no longer benefit our life. To become healthy and to respect ourselves and others, we need to relearn our negative emotional reactions to stress and anxiety which can trigger many unhealthy emotional responses.

If the artist constantly experiences pessimistic emotions for months or years, it can become a state of mind which traps us in a spin of negative emotions. Living in a despair state of mind alters the brain's thought processes and causes our perspective to be imbalanced. A gloomy mindset weakens the vitality of our physical health. Eventually, the creativity that makes up the essence of the artist resigns to inner turmoil. During this unsteady time, our supportive relationships may fracture, and our resilience in the artist's journey may snap. And there's no extra-hold hairspray, brown bobby pins, or magic glitter that can fix our melancholy emotions.

I have learned to give special attention to my inner world, my relationships, and my art.

Sometimes that means I need to spend time off stage, out of the limelight, to work on my emotional wounds and cognitive dissonance. While most of us want to be on the stage working our craft, waiting in the wings gives us an opportunity to soothe our emotions and strengthen our self-perspective.

Whenever turbulent emotions and inappropriate behaviors leap into my life, I ask myself: What is going on here? Is this a mood swing or a repetitive negative emotion? What is the source of this emotion? Am I afraid? Am I feeling insecure? Am I emotionally or physically in pain?

I ask trusted others: What's your view on my situation? Am I seeing all the facts? Is this the wise thing to do? Self-awareness comes from intentionally making yourself vulnerable to the possibility your emotions don't accurately reflect the truth of the situation. I may feel alone, but the truth is I have many friends who are there for me. The perspective of a friend might reveal a new insight and slow the emotional, dizzy spin to a steady panorama.

Once I've pinpointed what I feel and why, I look at my choices to respond. I try out different options and the possible results of my actions. What might happen if I talked to this person about their hurtful remark? What would happen if I discounted my pain and pretended everything was okay? What if I chose a passive-aggressive response and zinged a hurtful response at them? Which response would move me down an emotionally healthy path?

Working on a partnership between my emotions and logic enables me to step out from behind the curtain onto the stage. It's necessary not only to find that peaceful union within and with others, but also to gain emotional fortitude to conquer the many challenges of an artist's journey. It will help you endure the periods of inactivity and give you energy and appreciation for the success that will come your way.

In my dreams, I have the emotional stamina of an Irish dancer. I bounce around in a dashing Celtic dance outfit to highly spirited music. But the Irish dance, with its fast-moving steps, high kicks, and quick turns, would cause a blur of stress and imbalance. The pace is a bit too fast for me to be at my emotional best. The racing music would require substantial downtime to restore my equilibrium.

In reality, my emotional rhythm is more of a conga line—easygoing steps, low kicks, and slow turns. I work best when I have pauses between my activities to keep my emotions from doing a face-plant. And when life is hectic and I'm hearing the fast notes of an Irish violin, I have to plan space in my calendar to check and regain my emotional balance.

I'm learning to embrace my highly sensitive nature, allowing it to empower my writing and my creativity, all the while heeding the warning signals of emotions ruling my life. I desire to be authentic, crafting my own steps or pace for the marathon journey of an artist. Finding my emotional rhythm and intellectual flow takes me out of the wings onto the stage where art can be revealed in the best light.

Use the questions below to reflect on your current rhythm in life.

Dance Sequence

1. Find the song "Can't Stop the Feeling" by Justin Timberlake on YouTube. (I liked the Stormtroopers version.) Can you get up and dance? What dance depicts your current emotion?
2. Do you think you are a highly sensitive person? What characteristics do you have?
3. Do you have a habit of emotional self-care? What do you do? What steps do you need to incorporate?
4. Do you have healthy physical practices such as eating, exercise, or sleeping?
5. Do you find you need to withdraw during hectic weeks or months? Where do you go to find refreshment for your artist's soul?
6. Have you overextended yourself for others either emotionally or physically? Have you overextended yourself for the audience?
7. What steps do you need to make to get closer to emotional balance and health?
8. Name an artist whose emotional disarray negatively affected their career. What can you learn from their emotional missteps?

To plant a garden is to believe in tomorrow.
—Audrey Hepburn

Chapter 6
Blooming After a Storm

Most summer mornings, with a cup of coffee in hand, I walk out to my rose garden in the backyard. There I sit on the weathered white swing nestled among the flowers and listen to the bees seeking their daily portion. I watch hummingbirds darting around, making a quick assessment of the yard. I drink in the fruity aroma of my rambling white rose, Darlow's Enigma. I admire the light pink petals of the English rose, Heritage. This garden is a labor of love, for everything about the prairie and the High Plains' climate fights against the life of a rose.

Over a hundred years ago, the land which is now my backyard was a wind-whipped playground for rangeland animals. Deer, antelope, and buffalo fed on short spikes of grass that sprang from temperamental dirt. The hard-white clay soil moaned and cracked when dried by the sun, and rejoiced and glistened when saturated by a sporadic rain shower. The High Plains landscape, with its low moisture and high elevation, is considered a near desert terrain where cactus blooms from June rains, and the grass turns golden from the August heat.

Pioneers with a courageous dream walked along the dusty prairie trails of the High Plains just east of the Rocky Mountains.

Their wagons carried only essentials along the trail, plus a tenacious plant, called Harison's rose, which can still be seen growing along the Oregon Trail, nearby farms, and my childhood home. My grandmother brought the rose to Wyoming in the early 1920s. As a little girl, I enjoyed its beauty on the east side of the homestead where it bloomed in early summer on long, fountain-like canes that flowed with yellow sunshine, and its strong fragrance lingered in the yard like a good friend. My sisters and I carefully plucked the five-petal rose from its thorny stem and created a corsage for my mom to wear to church.

A few years ago, my mom sold the homestead. Numerous household items and farming equipment were auctioned. Cherished family memorabilia was bubble-wrapped and packed. The culmination of a hundred years of family life was loaded into a moving van, leaving behind the empty structures of house and barns. In this exodus, I didn't want to abandon Grandma's rose, the tough yellow rose which had grown along with our family. So I dug up a root and brought it to my yard. I planted it in a corner of my garden among other roses and flowers. I watered it. I spoke to the rose, encouraging it to grow and bloom again.

As I care for my grandma's rose, I ponder all that it had seen and endured in its ninety-plus years of existence: the harsh blizzards, the infertile soil, the severe droughts, and the intense hailstorms. Even in the midst of hardship, this amazing rose continues to spread its beauty and bloom. Only a resilient and tenacious rose can survive and thrive in Wyoming's difficult climate.

I draw strength from my rose garden as I persist on my artist's pilgrimage.

On this journey as an artist on a mission from God, I endure many wind-whipped days which try to topple me from the creative path. The storms test my artistic confidence and deepest beliefs. The soil of my artist life lacks food for my soul. A period of creative drought dries up my artistic vitality and fruitfulness. Weathered by inclement life circumstances, I wonder whether to quit the creative trail or find a safe shelter.

Greenhouse Effects

In the uncomplicated and perfect world, I want my artist's journey to resemble a plant's life in a large, ornate greenhouse. The glass structure guards against the destruction of hail or any violent weather. It shields my body of work from being flogged by various sizes of ice balls, leaving me stripped of beauty and confidence. The greenhouse's temperature, being regulated and temperate, could ease my artist's struggle to awaken from dormancy after a long cold spell. Seasons of creativity would be constant. The enclosure ensures I'd never be doubled over or dehydrated from gusting wind. The perfect amount of water, food, and sunshine nourishes my artist's soul. Innovative growth could be endless.

While the greenhouse protects from environmental foes, it also hinders pollination. The winds, which can dry and damage, are necessary for the plant to pollinate, flower, and produce seeds. Inside the greenhouse, the ventilation or fans may create a slight breeze, but it's usually not enough to carry the pollen of a stamen (male part) to the pistil (female part). Without wind, butterflies, or the birds and bees (*you didn't realize you would get a steamy sex story in an artist's book, did you?*), the plant's growth is thwarted.

Few plants spend their whole life in a greenhouse. In due time, most plants are transplanted outside the greenhouse and must learn to adapt to the variable and wacky ecosystem. It is outside the greenhouse, dealing with the challenging storms, the soil composition, the dormancy of winter, and the heat of summer, that a rose bush, or an artist, can grow and stretch to its maximum size. It is in leaving the protection and regulation of the greenhouse that the artist can develop resilience and tenacity.

Storm Resistant

Angela Duckworth, PhD, the leader in resilience research, and author of *Grit: The Power of Passion and Perseverance,* (2016), found that grit is the key to achieving long-term goals and successes. Her study revealed passion and perseverance outweigh a person's talent, intelligence, good looks, or income in the pursuit of success. Grit is about working hard at goals day after day, month after month, year after year, until the dreams are fully realized. It's not something you are born with. It's not something you can attain quickly. Grit is built one storm at a time.

Driving home after work on a main artery of the city, the rain pounds on the roof of my white family van. Suddenly, a trapdoor in the heavens releases hail stones the size of quarters, ambushing my vehicle. The hail falling on my van sounds like a catapult of stones thrown at a metal wall. The windshield wipers are doing their best to counterpunch the attacks. The van slides on hail piled like snow. Fearing an accident, I seek refuge in a Taco Bell parking lot under a few small crabapple trees. The barrage of hail strips through the branches and leaves, slowing the ice rock assault. I fear that the windshield will break, exposing me to the wicked strikes of the ice. My hands cover my ears muffling the mortar fire of hail. I cower down into my seat in the van, silently praying like a soldier in a foxhole.

After an eternity of fifteen minutes, the storm moves off to the east, the hail diminishes, and I resume my journey home. I notice cars with cracked windshields at the shopping mall and the broken windows of neighborhood houses. Once inside the safety of my home, I listen to the kids' stories of the hailstorm. We check our windows and skylight for cracks and seeping water. All is good. We are safe.

Finally, I peer through the patio door into the now dark

backyard trying to assess the damage. "How are m-my r-roses?"

"You probably shouldn't look at them tonight," my daughter Savannah replies with a hint of warning.

The soft morning light fails to minimize the harsh destruction in my backyard. The roses—which had been full of pregnant buds, just days from blooming and releasing their extravagant scent—are now mutilated green sticks protruding from the ground. With a rake and a compost bin, I gather the remnants of the rose plants. My gardener's heart feels like I'm walking through a graveyard of decapitated buds, bruised withered leaves, and broken stems.

This isn't the first hailstorm the prairie grasslands have endured in their history. But it is the first where its destruction affects something I poured my passion, creativity, and energy into. Usually a hailstorm produces pea-sized hail lasting a few minutes and has little effect on the plants. But this massive storm produces panic that my lovely roses will die and the beauty I labored to create will be erased.

Ten days after the storm, with the encouragement of the warm sun and consistent watering, the green stems grow new leaves.

A month after the storm, the rose bushes make a full recovery bearing new flower buds. In fact, the roses seem more vibrant after the storm.

Roses are considered delicate plants, and a few truly are. But the storm experience proves roses are tougher than they appear. The soft petals or dainty leaves can be deceptive, cloaking the rose bush's inner strength. Leaves and blooms reappear after a storm because they are the essence of a rose. Its identity is to grow green silky leaves and beautiful fragrant flowers. A typical storm can't destroy a rose's identity or purpose. In fact, as ugly and stressful as a storm can be, it may also be the catalyst which brings a resilient rose into abundant beauty.

Storms on our artist's journey will cause us to question if we are talented enough, or smart enough or profitable enough to achieve our artistic objectives. We will be tempted to give up on our dreams and goals. If we withstand the first storm, there will be another. And then another. That's life outside the safe but sterile greenhouse. How do we keep the stormy seasons from toppling us from the artistic journey?

Duckworth's research shows that resilience is sustained by belief—a mindset of what is true about our identity and strengths as artists. When a difficulty appears on our artist's path, it tests our beliefs in who we are and what we can do. In the process of overcoming the challenge, we may find some of our beliefs are false. For example, after a disappointing art show where the judge picked apart your painting, you realize watercolors aren't a strength or a passion; that you are doing it just because it's your grandma's passion. A storm will strip us bare so that only the beliefs that serve us well can sprout. For instance, after the eighty-fifth theater audition, you get a callback because the previous eighty-four tryouts taught that you are great at depicting horror characters.

With each challenge, there is an opportunity to have a growth mindset. Each problem demands a different skillset to try and use. As you learn what works and what doesn't work, you feel more in control of the outcomes, and your self-confidence increases. For example, the steps to publish a book can feel like one windy squall after another. With each step, a writer could give up. But a gritty writer draws on other the experience of other writers, learns about the process, and tackles it the best they can. Later, when it's time to publish the second book, the writer has increased confidence and resilience.

So storms are good. They don't feel good. In fact, they suck. Without storms, we won't develop the inner strength, the grit, to persevere. Storms cause us to solidify our beliefs about our artist's identity and grow through the failures or challenges. Storms happen above ground, but there is more that happens to our resilience below the surface.

The Soil Where You Are Planted

Many years ago, I moved into a house and property which was in rough shape. It had old carpet, faded paint, and a barren backyard. The previous owner had good intentions of cultivating a rose garden in the yard. All that existed was a square piece of off-white clay dirt cut out of the weedy lawn surrounded by thirsty prairie.

The first time I went out to dig a hole in the barren square, my shovel only penetrated six inches into the hard clay soil. Using my weight to stand on a shovel, or even stab with a hoe, only dented the antagonistic soil. It was more like chiseling rock than designing a garden. I filled the six-inch hole with water, hoping the ground would soften. The liquid just sat there in the shovel-carved cup of clay. I soon realized that clay soil is water resistant and slow to drain. An hour passed before the clay absorbed the water and softened enough allowing me to dig down another six inches and finally break through the clay crust. That was the routine whenever I planted a rose bush. Not fun, not easy, not for the impatient or easily deterred!

For a beautiful rose bush to thrive, the troublesome clay dirt needs to change to a nutrient-rich soil. The clay dirt is alkaline in nature, and while perfect for the potter or sculptor, it opposes the acid-loving, water-needing roots of the rose.

When I plant a rose, I add sand to break up the clotting clay soil and enable water to drain. I also add a shovel of pure steer manure, yes, pure crap—a seemly oxymoron but that's what was written on the bag—to the soil. In the spring and summer, I water, apply rose fertilizer, and pull out the strangling weeds. I nurture these gorgeous plants. In the fall, I add a layer of compost, decomposed matter which adds nutrients, around the existing plants. Complete change in the soil doesn't happen in one summer. Or in two summer seasons. Slowly and steadily, over the years, as I keep adding supplements to the soil, it evolves. With better soil, each rose's vitality of bloom and stature improves.

As a gardener and plant artist. I know roses are influenced by the dirt. The richness of soil determines the size and color of a rose. They thrive or struggle according to the degree of adaptability to the environment. I can imagine an English rose, bred for the fertile soil conditions of Britain, looking around at the Wyoming prairie and thinking: *Oh no, growing and blooming here is impossible. It's too dry. Or too sticky. It's just too deficient in nutrients.*

To which I respond: *Oh yes, my pretty, it's true that there will be bad soil. But it's also a fact that with attention, the soil will become fertile. And you will change the barren landscape with your uncommon beauty.*

My level of resistance or acclimation to where I'm planted plays a huge part in my grittiness and success. Change in my life can be as slow, hard, and defiant as clay soil. The breaking down of negative perceptions about where I live can be as difficult as penetrating the clay crust. It can be both uncomfortable and necessary as I, the artist, adjust to my fluctuating external environment of difficult work situations or endless family demands. Often, transition can shock the system, paralyzing my motivation, therefore requiring help from outside forces. Sometimes change happens in the glow of sunlight as I embrace the evolution and go willingly.

As artists, our ability to adapt to where we are planted depends on flexible thinking, realistic positivity, and behavior modification. This can apply directly to where we live or to our creative performance. Inflexible or rigid thinking says it should only be done this way. We use words like "never" or "always." When we tell ourselves, *people in this town are never going to get my art,* we have just talked ourselves out of creating. We fail to grow through the challenge of communicating with our audience.

Let's say a vocalist performs a song and struggles with pitch, especially on a high note. Rigid thinking would utter: *My per-*

formance was horrible. I'm a terrible vocalist and I'm never going to sing again. But flexible thinking declares: *I sometimes struggle with a few notes, but my voice was strong on the rest of the song. I'll work on it for next time.* Hear the difference? Our inner voice can direct us quit or go forward.

With flexible thinking, comes realistic optimism. Looking around at our landscape helps us diagnose the facts about the challenges. Is there something I can do to improve my current situation? What skills need focus and mastery? What people do I need to be around to find motivation? Are there groups where I can share my artistry?

Flexible thinking patterns and realistic optimism are key ingredients to changing the soil where we are rooted. When we view failures as momentary, we seek to adapt new work habits, new skills, or new perspectives which transform our creative garden in which we live. It won't happen overnight. It may not happen in a year. But consistently approaching our goals with new perspectives, positive outlooks, and positive behavior give us the perseverance to step forward in our artistic journey.

Drought and Stamina

I look closely at the rose petals. The edges are brown and curled. During a hot, dry summer, as much as I water the roses, the blooms still wilt. Living at sixty-two-hundred-feet elevation, the sun is intense. I can feel it penetrating my arms and face. And so can the rose. At high altitude, people and plants are exposed to sixty percent more sun than at sea level. While a rose needs the sun, it can also burn the flowers. A rose needs a lot of sun, but the sun can also damage the delicate rose petals.

Before I plant a rose, I research whether they do better in full sun, or partial shade. There is a strategy for planting a rose where it can best thrive. As an artist, having a strategy for our journey is also needed.

After leaving my creative and fulfilling job of leading artists, I found a job as a bank teller. I had been a teller in my early twenties, so returning to the position was familiar. I looked at the job as short-term, something to financially support my family until I found an art-related job I would enjoy. My new job was at the largest and busiest bank in town. It required hours of prolonged focus on money transactions, a temperament for dealing with a variety of people, and strenuous time on my feet. While being friendly with customers was easy for me, the details of numbers were not.

For as long as I can remember, mathematical tasks have been my adversary. Numbers have played tricks on me, changed positions, or just disappeared from my thoughts. When I had to recall historical dates, or when I counted things or added up inches, my mind became a sink hole (*was it fifty-four bottles of beer or fifty-six?*). To process financial transactions, I had to concentrate. It was easy to enter in a wrong check amount or miscount cash and coins.

The pressure of accuracy was immense. It was the bank's policy to fire a teller who had had a yearly cumulative cash error totaling two hundred dollars. If a teller didn't pay attention, a two-hundred-dollar error often happened in one transaction, a mere moment of distraction. At first, I focused on keeping my cash and checks in balance. After five years, I became the senior teller with more responsibilities, such as balancing the vault and the bank branch.

On a very busy Friday, after closing the bank's front door, I was balancing the branch's numbers. The numbers didn't equal each other. We were fifty cents short. Fifty cents? To find two thousand dollars—a bundle of twenty-dollar bills—or ten thousand dollars—a bundle of one-hundred-dollar bills—was much easier to find than fifty lousy cents.

A colleague and I recounted all the wrapped coins, bags of coins, and straps of cash in the vault but still had the fifty cents off. The branch's closing procedures were only supposed to take fifteen minutes. An hour and a half later, after calling our supervisor to come back to double check our work, the fifty cents were still missing. Finally, we accepted failure and closed the bank branch with a shortage. If it had been my bank account, I would have just subtracted the fifty cents from my total and gone out for a glass of wine. But that's not the way of the banking world! A financial institution out of balance is like stealing from the customer and is reported to the money gods who then investigate and require more counting.

As I drove home, my mind replayed the events of the last few hours. "Yes, René, your life sucks," I shouted aloud to the universe. Tears of frustration and hopelessness blurred my eyes as despair filled my heart. The Friday night balancing disaster was one of many I had endured over the past couple of years. I hated having a job that was neither interesting nor invigorating. And it wasn't just that I was uninterested and bored, but the way of the bank's culture left me exhausted.

My mind and body were depleted from having to labor from my mathematical weakness rather than my inborn creative strengths. The corporate landscape of numbers and policies fought against my natural artistic instincts. My search for a job that better fit my artistic abilities and passions had been met with a multitude of rejections. I was at an impasse. I was chained at the stake of a meaningless job which squeezed out every bit of life-nectar I had and then some. I didn't have the motivation to sketch or write or pursue anything creative. Day after day, I forced myself to go to work, stay at work, and focus on my work. I felt scorched and withered. My soul, along with any artistic aspirations, gasped for breath as I died a slow death.

A few weeks later, I attended the company Christmas party. Part of the holiday festivities was drawing for various prizes—a camera, a microwave, a flat-screen TV, and a laptop to name a few. The people at my table were joking around, not paying much attention to the drawing. Someone from another table leaned over and shouted above the noise, "René, they called your name."

"What?"

The Christmas spirit at my table hindered my hearing.

"You won the laptop." She cheerfully pointed to the front of the room where the lady with the microphone was still calling my name.

I was ecstatic! Not only because it was a new Dell laptop, but I knew it was a sign I *was* supposed to write a book. Now I *had* to find time to write.

My youngest daughter was in dance classes twice a week, all the way downtown, too far to drop off and go back home. At first, I wasted my time drinking coffee and looking at magazines at a coffee shop near the dance studio. Having won the laptop meant I was able write on the go, taking it with me to the coffee shop. While my daughter danced, I would write. Surrounded by rows of books on oak shelves, and breathing in the earthy fragrances of coffee, I wrote about my experiences as a leader of artists.

At the time, it didn't matter whether I knew how to write a book. Writing for a couple of hours on Tuesdays and Thursdays became a way of watering the soil of my life, allowing for a new perspective of my artist's journey. The writing sessions allowed me to escape from the corporate world and reflect on my creative past with humor and appreciation. I wrote for the pure fun of experimenting with voice and style. As the words formed paragraphs, I experienced my creative roots elongating and gripping the new fertile ground. Writing about my artistic experiences, reminded me of who I really was despite the job I held. Gradually the lethargic and impotent soil of my life changed. My focus was no longer on the unsatisfying job, but on the next chapter of the book, the next step in my artist's path.

I stole time away to write, hiding away at the library or coffee shop on days other than when my daughter had dance lessons. I even called in sick to work to attend a writer's conference. I reclaimed power over my life. Although my job landscape didn't change, I could endure the crazy workdays as my artistic nature took root and engaged again with the artist's journey. Any gardener knows it's the balance of water and sun which keeps the roots alive. Sometimes, it's a daily sprinkle, sometimes we need the full-on irrigation of creativity to revive our artist's soul.

A strategy for accomplishing our artistic goals is crucial to passion and perseverance on our artist's journey. Intentionally planning your creative activities focuses your daily steps, your monthly strides, and your yearly wins. There's no magic to strategy other than having a plan of action and putting art activities on your calendar. I make sure I don't go two weeks without writing or engaging in a creative event.

When we realize we can make daily choices which influence our goals, we regain our purpose and develop grit. Basking in the daily wins, or weekly triumphs, refocuses our efforts. It makes us responsible for our journey. It builds our resilience.

In the artist's journey, it's personal resiliency that brings us through periods of storms and revives the eagerness to be authentic to our creative genetics. Having an unfulfilling job kept me from being complacent. If I had been in a job that fit my talents and interests, I wouldn't have been desperate to figure out my purpose in life. It was the messiness of the personal storm that caused me to find ways to soak my creative roots with writing sessions and conferences. It was caring for my creative soul that gave me the ability to stand up after being wind-whipped and bent over.

At the end of our workweek, we are responsible to thrive, to explore, and to develop goals and strategies for our artistry. The corporation we work for isn't responsible for that. As artists we may find a job that fits our creative abilities and get paid for it—an artist's greenhouse scenario. For most of us, it may not happen. The full extent of our artistry may exist outside the greenhouse in the flux of inclement weather, planted in creatively deprived soil. Challenges to create art will hamper us only if we let it and give up. Like the rose, storms may strip us of our usual growth, but it is only for a short time. With a strong root system and a little sunshine, we can regain our artistic vitality. To walk through a creative storm doesn't have to destroy us as artists. Instead it can be the catalyst that propels us with stubborn eagerness to be more than we ever imagined we would be: a thriving, vibrant artist, an uncommon beauty planted in the midst of the prairie.

Use the questions below to evaluate your creative landscape.

The Creative Landscape

1. Are you planted in a place where you can flourish?
2. What hinders your artistic growth? What creative elements do you need to add to help you flourish?
3. What are your self-perceptions that need to be challenged and/or altered?
4. Where can you be planted to receive creative influence?
5. Are you enduring a storm or drought in your artist life? What can you do to rebloom after the storm?
6. Are you a resilient artist? Why? Why not?
7. Buy a plant, water it, fertilize it, and watch it grow. Let it symbolize your artist's journey. (Unless it dies, then buy another plant, like a succulent or a cactus, which you basically can't kill!)

Leaders must encourage their organizations to dance to forms of music yet to be heard.
—Warren G. Bennis

Chapter 7
Composing My Leadership Music Suite

Prelude—Tempo Rubato—Expressive with the Rhythmic Freedom of Artists

I enjoy my running routine, and today is no different. The sun peeks between the bent arms of wind-blown trees teasing me with the potential of another day. As I look down the dusty street, the strong mixture of summer odors—wet grass and purple lilacs—fills my lungs. I scan through the songs on my phone, looking for something to fit my mood. I don't feel like listening to country, or 80s rock music. I toggle past Lynyrd Skynyrd and land on an instrumental movie score written by Bryan Adams and Hans Zimmer.

As I start my run, I casually listen to the music as my stride matches the rhythm. The harmony and movement of the individual instruments of one particular soundtrack snap me out of my runner's trance. The snare drum begins the piece with a beat that mimics the sound of running horses. The string instruments join the drums, laying the groundwork with long smooth notes. The French horn, trombone, and baritone horn take the first turn at the melody, creating anticipation, and then move to the background of the composition. The piano takes the solo, playing the simplistic yet rich melody, slowly and deliberately creating a crescendo. As the whole orchestra joins in, there is a rousing climax of the musical suite. Unexpectedly, tears form in my eyes. The beauty of the musical score kidnaps me from my daily plodding. It takes me from my ordinary existence and transports me to the top of an invigorating mountain cliff. I can see it with my mind's eye and sense it with my soul. Usually, I admire the poetry of well-written lyrics, but at this moment, it isn't words that lift me into another reality. In the absence of words, it is the emotion of the instruments played by musicians that captures me.

For the rest of the run, I speculate on the relationship between the musicians and their conductor who performed the music. *Was it an enjoyable and encouraging relationship? What challenges had they overcome together? Did the leader have a negative or positive influence on the musical collaboration?*

I had a high school band teacher who enjoyed whipping around her authoritative white baton. One time she was banging her baton on the music stand in front of her, trying to get the saxophones to play their notes in sync with the rest of us. She suddenly lost her grip, sending the pointed wand flying past one musician's head. It came within inches of his right eye. We sat there stunned, protecting our own eyes, as she picked up her weapon. She was frustrated with the saxophone players' lack of musical ability. She retrieved her baton and used it to point at them. "You can put your instruments away. You are done distracting the rest of the band."

With sagging shoulders and downcast eyes, the two musicians got up from their chairs and quietly tucked their saxophones away in their black cases. They stood at the back while we went through the song one last time before a tinny bell shrilled, ending the class.

I was horrified at the public shaming of my fellow musicians and appalled at the display of frustration by the band teacher. I thought she should have behaved better, more patient and loving. After all, she's the adult mentor, and we were mere teenage students.

Years later, I recalled that negative band experience as I sat in a gymnasium anticipating the basketball game between crosstown rivalries and observed a captivating musical display between a conductor and musicians.

The band was grouped five rows deep and eight to ten musicians wide on the bleachers in the lower corner of the muggy gym. They were playing a lively pop tune and swaying, almost dancing, to the song. I looked for the conductor. He wasn't standing in front as usual, but to the left side of the band. His hips bounced to the same beat the musicians played, and while he waved his baton to lead the group, it wasn't needed. It seemed both the conductor and the musicians heard an inner meter that symbiotically held them together. The connection between the musicians and the music was dynamic. The music was life-giving and drew me in. Again, I wondered about the relationship between the conductor and the musicians. A search of the high school's website allowed me to find the band leader's email and set up a time to meet with him.

The laughter and conversations move me forward down the halls of East High School. Peeking in a classroom door window, I see students standing around, flirting, talking, and laughing. School had dismissed fifteen minutes earlier, but the band room still held ten lively kids.

"Are you looking for Mr. Holroyd?" a smiling, sixteen-ish boy holding drumsticks asks me.

"Yes." I nod, looking around the large band room for any sign of a large-and-in-charge teacher.

"He's in there." He points with his drumstick at a door on the right side of the band room.

"Just knock and go in," he continues to direct me. "He's there."

So I knock and hear a man's voice. "Come in."

Dressed in khaki pants and a knit vest with a white shirt, Mr. Dan Holroyd leans back in his office chair. Another music teacher sits opposite of Dan and I feel I disrupted their discussion. I sit down at a coworker's desk and look around the closet-sized room as the two teachers finish their conversation. The gray cinderblock walls peek between eight-by-eleven-inch pictures of East High bands in various locations. Most are of tropical locations with palm trees and oceans in the background. The teacher leaves, and Dan turns his attention to me.

"So tell me, why do you lead the high school band?" I ask.

"I believe playing in a band helps students personally grow and succeed in life," Dan begins. "Learning to play a musical instrument can bring lifelong enjoyment."

Dan explained that while a math or English teacher may have a student for one year, a band teacher often has a student for all four years of high school. For those four years, his goal for his students isn't just for them to become better musicians and enjoy creating music for a lifetime. Dan's primary goal for those participating in band is to find a place to belong in an artistic community.

Allemande—A Stately Dance, Leading with Arms Interlinked

Many parents have informed Dan that being a part of the band helped their child through high school and graduation. Many students have also told Dan that being in the band enabled them to show up to school and tolerate their required classes. One girl came into the music room, sat down in her chair, and said, "Finally, band!"

Several years ago, while at an awards ceremony for one of my daughters, I witnessed Dan's induction into the East High School Hall of Fame. In his acceptance speech, he told how as a high school student, he needed a place to belong. Now as a band teacher, that experience motivates him to create a place where the band isn't just about perfectly playing music. It's about creating a safe place for his pupils to connect to each other.

The hum of happy kids outside Dan's office brings me back to the band room. Most teachers would have shooed them away a few minutes after the school day ended. To me, the vibration of student laughter is evidence they have found a safe place to explore both music and friendships.

To bring out the best in his musicians, Dan claims they must want to play for each other. That only happens when they are invested in each other's lives. He creates a classroom culture based on mutual respect, accountability, and empowerment. This occurs not only within the high school building, but in the cosmopolitan classrooms outside those school walls.

Every two years, Dan plans a trip for the band to travel outside of Wyoming. The band travels to a destination and performs their music at various venues. They have gone to Hawaii and the Bahamas. Next year, Dan plans on taking the band to New York City. It's designed to be a holistic experience for the teenagers as they encounter other cultures, live with their bandmates, and perform music in unique settings. For many, it's their first experience beyond their local community. Most have never seen the ocean or a building over two stories tall. On one trip, a student stared up to the sky and asked, "What's that tall plant with large leaves?"

"It's a palm tree!" Dan quipped with a smile.

For Dan's accomplishments with his students, East High School, and the musical community at large, he was awarded Outstanding Director for Wyoming in 2015. As a leader among high school conductors, Dan wrote an article about the importance of developing community within the music room. Other music teachers around the state have also latched on to developing relationships and artistic community among the musicians. Dan's ability to create a sense of trust and fun among students in the band has transformed the teens' lives, both musically and personally.

Before I met Dan Holroyd, I read a story about artists and

community. In the late 1890s to the early 1900s, artists gathered in Paris, the art center of the world. Paris had the art institutes and museums that drew dedicated artists to learn, grow, and perhaps display their creativity. Pablo Picasso and Henri Matisse often gathered for dinner, allowing the painters to form mutual respect. They met regularly at each other's studios to enjoy tea and critique each other's latest paintings. They discussed their views of not only art, but their passions for religion and politics. Often the conversations over food included French pianist and composer Claude Debussy and the newest shining musician, Igor Stravinsky. The artists forged friendships which expanded their creativity and profession. This inspired me as a creative director and leader of artists to make a change.

At a staff meeting, I told my peers I aimed to develop a stronger bond between the artists by asking them to spend extra time together.

"Are you sure you need to do this?" challenged one leader.

"The artists are too busy getting the work done to spend extra time together," stated another coworker.

"Don't artists prefer to be alone?" someone sarcastically suggested.

Despite all the negativity, I knew in order for a group of artists to realize their potential, I needed to be intentional about creating a place of trust, belonging, and fun.

At first, I started small, something safe and less intrusive. We attended a movie and afterwards discussed it over pie at the local Shari's. Then we read a book on creativity and discussed our impressions of the book at a local coffee shop. Sometimes we just hung out at someone's house eating barbecue and talking about life.

As it often happens in a creative brainstorming group, there was a disagreement over a proposed idea between a few artists. My brain went on full alert. I knew the emergency drill like a rat running the familiar maze. I had been through way too many conflicting ideas, which led to conflicting artists, which led to some kind of personnel explosion, which resulted with an artist leaving the team.

This time, something remarkable happened. Rather than the usual defensiveness, the person who had thrown the idea out to the group asked questions: *"Tell me why you're hesitant about the idea?"* Or, *"What could we do to make the idea better?"* Or even, *"It's just an idea. I'm cool with whatever meets our goal."*

The togetherness outside the workspace influenced what was happening inside the workspace. Trust and friendship built through our community time allowed the artists to feel secure in the disagreement. The group became a safe place to artistically explore. The artist, who gave a part of herself in her idea, now realized each teammate cared for her. Based on the foundation of authentic friendships, she respected their perspective enough to want to listen to their viewpoint. Potential artist explosion aborted.

Leaders of artists who want their creatives to thrive must build a trusted community where the synergetic combustion of innovation can occur. Since creativity incorporates the whole person, the artist must feel comfortable for imagination to be accessed and unleashed. When trust and security increase through interpersonal relationships, an intoxicating chemistry happens among the artists. They get each other's jokes, half sentences, and hand gestures. They understand and respect each other's roles as they share the same passions and challenges. The synergy of the group causes the creativity to burst past the usual boundaries to an unquantifiable and unpredictable quadrant.

I wonder if Picasso and Matisse had a premonition, as they sipped tea and critiqued each other's paintings, of the influence they were having on each other and the colorful revolution they were igniting. I wonder if Stravinsky knew the truthfulness of his mentor Debussy and the creativity of his friend Picasso would propel him to become the most influential composer of the twentieth century. I wonder if the students in band class realized Dan Holroyd's positive leadership fostered artistic friendships that made them better musicians and young adults.

I wonder if these artists knew as they supported each other's creativity, challenged each other's artistry, and collaborated on each other's works that they were about to change their artistic future. Most of us artists won't live in Paris, or have Debussy as a mentor, or have Matisse as a painting partner. But all of us can be a trailblazer for building relationships and stimulating innovation with other artists.

While the artist may resist and may want to work alone, connection with other artists is crucial to our creative journey. Communities of artists are the allies which support and encourage us on the long and difficult road. They point out the pitfalls of our work. They cheer our accomplishments. They lift us up when we want to quit the artist's journey. It's in linking arms with these valuable relationships that offer a place of belonging where we can release the powerful synergy of creativity.

Minuet—Tempo Giusto (Leading at the "Right" Speed)

"It's tough to be a music teacher, lead the band, and maintain playing my instrument," admits Dan.

Sitting in Dan's office, where leaning stacks of music books and sheet music stand two feet tall, we're discussing the challenge of balancing leadership and artistry.

"But I need to be a good example for my band kids. I tell them that playing an instrument is a skill to enjoy throughout life, so I have to make time to do that myself."

Dan is a percussionist and enjoys performing with the Cheyenne Orchestra, a jazz band at a local restaurant, and the community band. He can enjoy his artistry because of his mentoring system for young artist leaders in the band.

Developing a leadership structure within the band is essential to empowering students. Dan chooses the student leader based on maturity and people skills. They don't have to be the best musician. In fact, the first chair, the best musician in the section, usually doesn't have the leadership abilities. The student leaders go through a leadership training course which outlines expectations. Each section, like percussion or brass, has a leader who is accountable for the group's musical proficiency and interpersonal relationships. If there are personal conflicts, the section leader is obligated to intervene and help the musicians resolve their differences. The section leaders answer to the drum major and then to Dan. The goal for the leadership structure is to raise up student leaders who can guide the band if Dan isn't there. Delegating leadership responsibilities to students not only prepares them to become future leaders in the community, but allows Dan to grow as a conductor and musician. It helps bring balance between Dan the leader and Dan the artist.

"I wish I would have learned this sooner," I tell Dan. "I nearly burned out when I led my artists' teams, especially during the holiday season."

When people were thinking about Halloween, my creative team and I were brainstorming ideas for Christmas Eve services. While friends and family were watching football and baking sugar cookies, we were rehearsing. On Christmas Eve, while kids were impatient for Santa to arrive, we were performing for their parents so they could feel the love and joy of Christmas.

By our fourth and final Christmas Eve performance, I was annoyed by the slow, quiet songs telling me that "all is calm." All HAD NOT been calm in my life for about three months! Singing the song over and over was like the squeaking of a clarinet played by a young musician. I envied the joyfulness on people's faces as they rushed home to a buttery and juicy turkey dinner that would make Martha Stewart proud. My family gathered in the bleak green room with a Christmas wreath on the door and ate cold deli sandwiches. After the stressful months of leading, I was an avatar with green hairy skin, and the only Christmas song I sang was "You're a mean one, Mr. Grinch."

On Christmas mornings I was usually sneezing or coughing

to the tune of "Jingle Bells." As I watched the kids unwrap their gifts I had wrapped at midnight, I would whine about how tired I was. I knew joy had left my world and I didn't like it.

I used to be obsessed with completing my task list. It's the curse of my type "A" personality. Every morning, I made my list and I hated leaving anything unfinished. Often when I crossed off one thing on my list, two more tasks magically appeared. There were always new procedures to be implemented, reports to be printed, meetings to sleep through, and weekly duties to delegate. The tasks of a leader were endless.

I was slow to admit the pressure and demands of leadership had a negative impact on my creative nature. I felt stretched and pulled between doing the tasks that had to be done and taking care of my mental and physical health. As an artist and a leader, I had to feel the painful dissonance in my soul before I started to explore ways to bring harmony to my work and health.

One Monday morning, after that exhausting Christmas season, I turned off my phone and pushed pause on external distracting noises and internal nagging expectations. I sat down with my journal and examined the tempo of my life. *What was motivating this fast cadence in my life? Whose melody am I trying to imitate?* I wrote, drank tea, and wrote some more. Journaling has a way of decoding personal angst into legible truth.

Pausing my busy life to contemplate these questions led to some uncomfortable answers. This time of introspection allowed me to identify unhealthy leadership rationale and behaviors. Motivational speaker and sales mentor Zig Ziglar said, "You can't lead others if you can't lead yourself." If I let them, others' expectations can lead me. Distorted motivations can lead me. Pride or selfishness can lead me. Before I can be a positive influence on others, it's vital I'm directing the well-being of my own life first. Establishing health and balance of the inner self is the best way to impact others.

Daniel Goleman, researcher and author on emotion intelligence, described self-awareness benefits and contributions to high performance leaders. According to Goleman (2006), "Emotional intelligence is the ability to perceive emotions, to access and generate emotions so as to assist thought, to understand emotions and emotional knowledge, and to reflectively regulate emotions so as to promote emotional and intellectual growth." Goleman concluded, a leader with a high level of EI creates a culture of trust, healthy risk-taking, and learning, while low levels of EI produces anxiety and fear. Increasing our EI depends upon self-awareness, accurate self-assessment, and self-confidence.

It all begins with self-awareness—to have an honest perception of our moods and how they impact others. Naming our feelings generates a healthy understanding of ourselves. It gives us information on how we respond to stress, or joy, or sadness, or love. Connecting to our emotions is key to realizing how emotions affect our thoughts and decisions. This assessment enables self-knowledge and proactive strategies when leading others.

Without self-awareness, we can falsely judge our own abilities. You think you're a fantastic team leader, but your team quietly voices their frustration after you leave a meeting. Or you see yourself as a poor communicator, so you overcompensate with stupid jokes which disconnects the audience from your message and diminishes your influence. Both miss the mark of accurate self-knowledge and produce negative leadership behaviors. In an article on *Harvard Business Review*, research of Fortune 10 companies found leaders lacking self-awareness increases the likelihood of making worse decisions, engaging less in team coordination, and showing less conflict management abilities (Erich C. Dierdorff and Robert S. Rubin, March 12, 2015).

Accuracy in self-knowledge is significant because it is the baseline of our confidence. Gathering growth-oriented feedback from your team or friends gives insight to your strengths and weaknesses as a leader. And from this feedback you can know for sure what you're good at. Precisely and honestly viewing our abilities focuses our energy on our strengths. And causes us to figure how to deal with our shortcomings.

After that exhausting Christmas season many years ago, I wrote paragraphs that chronicled a new rhythm, a change in how I wanted to approach my leadership and artistry. *What are my best leadership abilities? How could I lead in a more efficient manner? What should I delegate, what should I do? What is reasonable for me to accomplish in a day? A week? A month? A year? Is it possible to slow down my pace, even create a complete pause or intermission and yet be an effective leader? How many creative events do I need to schedule to keep my artist's soul singing?*

I asked for feedback from my teams on my leadership. They loved my enthusiasm, vision-casting, team-building, and creative liberties given to the artists. However, I lost track of event details and timelines which caused confusion and uncertainty in their creative tasks. None of this shocked me. I was very aware of my lack of administrative skills. It didn't devastate me. In fact, it gave me freedom. I gave away the checklist of event details to a few artists who thrived in that arena so that I focused on creative vision and team-building. Relinquishing the need to do it all, I gained space to participate in soul-refreshing creativity.

Over the years I have collected Christmas snow globes. My favorite globe is a scene of a frosty New England country town with an old white church. I love to wind up the music box, shake the snow, and imagine being a part of the peaceful setting. The music box plays the delicate melody of "Silent Night." And for about two minutes, I believe *all is calm, all is quiet.* Slowly as it unwinds, the musical notes slow and then stop. Winding it, I again enjoy the melody, but this time as it slows, I wind it before it stops. The music is almost uninterrupted.

Like my snow globe, I need to pursue ways to keep my soul's melody playing. I have to train myself to listen, hearing when the notes are slowing down, and be prepared to rewind before it comes to an absolute stop. Dead silence has happened to my soul. Sometimes I haven't even noticed for a few days or weeks that the melody has stopped. But the more sensitive I am to my soul, the more I am able to realize when the notes are slowing and rewind, refresh, and renew.

I have witnessed leaders who have worked so hard that they forgot about their soul and spirit. They didn't realize that the notes were slowing until the music had stopped. And it didn't play a melody again for months, and sometimes years. The deadness of their soul led to depression, nervous breakdowns, addictions, and broken relationships. By ignoring their soul, they forgot their most precious song.

Sarabande—A Leader's Dance of Inherent Beauty, Allegretto Grazioso

John Quincy Adams said, "If your actions inspire others to dream more, learn more, do more, and become more, you are a leader."

As a leader, I have the opportunity to create a culture that brings out the best in artists. And it depends on balancing two key factors of management: people and creative product. It takes patience and foresight to handle both gracefully.

While in a local trendy clothing store, I happened upon a woman I had worked with when I was a creative director. As we caught up on kids and jobs, I asked Linda if she was still using her creative gifts. At first, Linda claimed she was too busy. When I recalled some of the unique contributions she made on several creative projects we did together, her eyes watered and she hung her head. She confided the pain she suffered with her current creative director.

Linda and the director worked on planning a stage design for an upcoming big event.

Linda left the meeting thinking she clearly understood the vision of the director for the project.

Her team jumped passionately into their assignment. They brainstormed ideas, looked at revamping existing props, and purchased new materials. Linda described it as an exhilarating creative experience.

The stage design team went early to set up the stage props and then headed to the lobby to decorate the area. During this activity, a few team members heard angry shouts in the auditorium. Team members peeked through the doorway to see the director ordering people to tear down the stage design they had just put up.

Shocked at the destruction of her creativity and hard work, Linda ran onto the stage and confronted the director, "What is going on?"

"It looks awful and now I to have to fix it." His voice shook with anger.

Intimidated by his enraged outburst, Linda left him to rip apart the stage and any trust she had in him.

According to Linda, this wasn't the first time the manager behaved unprofessionally and disrespectfully toward others. In the short duration of his position, Linda had observed others crumbling in the presence of the director's anger. It was understood among the artists in his department to avoid the director whenever he sulked or was in a bad mood.

A few days after the performance, Linda left a phone message for the director. She asked to meet with him to resolve the staging issue and mend their relationship. He never returned her phone call. Linda decided to shield herself from further being hurt and embarrassed and backed away.

In my friend's story, several things hit a sour note. First, the leader determined the creative product was more important than the person or team who put it together.

As a leader I have struggled to balance the value of both artist and their creative results. Often, I favored the artist over their art. I failed to address the sub-par quality of their art to protect the artist's ego and myself. My insecurities kept me from having a difficult conversation with the artist which only hindered their creative growth and excellence.

On the other hand, as in the story, for a leader to put more emphasis on the art, is disrespectful to the artist. The director told Linda it looked awful and embarrassed the team in front of others. Always, always, always confront another person in private. Shaming a person doesn't not change behavior. It only creates fear and distrust in the relationship. A leader will have many difficult conversations. It's part of leadership. Learning communication skills to resolve conflict is essential to any leader's success and influence.

Second, if the art product didn't coincide with expectations, then the leader has to own the failing as well. I have to question my communication of the vision or goal to the artist. Was it clear? Was I fuzzy on the expectations? Did I effectively follow up or check on the progress? If the art unexpectedly ended up somewhere than I intended, then I didn't lead well and need to take responsibility for the team's final product.

Finally, perhaps the creative project is flat because I didn't pair it with the right artist. When delegating projects, I can choose anyone. But not everyone will do the best job. During the team discussion on the project, I look for the artist who is talking fast with glazed eyes and drool running down their chin. This artist has the project already created in their mind.

Their passion will infuse the project with hard work and excellence.

Gigue Finale—The Leader's Fast Closing Dance

Over the span of my lifetime, I have attended many concerts. Some of them were beautifully done, some were not. Many concerts were so exhilarating that my body and soul swayed with the musical brilliance. I didn't want to leave the auditorium and hummed the tune long after the concert ended. Although I can't remember every note, the whole experience is unforgettable, transcendental to my soul.

Then there were concerts so poorly performed that I winced at the awkward notes and cringed at the unrecognizable melodies. I counted the exit signs and the bald heads seated in front of me, then contemplated what to order at Dairy Queen. The only way to forget the atrocious music was with a sugar buzz.

Our leadership will leave the artists we directed with a memory. They will not remember every word we said, or every motivational speech we gave, but they will remember how we made them feel. We will either leave them with impressions of exhilaration or boredom, transformation or stagnation, encouragement or criticism. They will recall the relationships which detracted or added to their creative lives. They will call to mind whether our leadership valued them as artists, or used them to produce art. The artist will instinctively know whether we balanced our leadership and artistry by the notes of our melody. They will remember the whole experience as if our leadership was a music suite played before their artistic lives. We could end up seeing them dancing to the captivating tune or have them covering their ears to silence the clanging noise they endured under our leadership.

Take a moment to remove yourself from your concert and sit in the audience with other artists.

Conversational Notes

1. Have you developed a community of artists of safety and trust? Are there steps to building an artist's community learned from Dan Holroyd's story which you can apply to your current situation?
2. Are you involved in a community of like-minded artists?
3. Is there a dissonance in your leadership soul? What areas of self-awareness, self-knowledge, and confidence will bring you to a sense of harmony?
4. Is there a clear melody of vision for your artistic teams? Is

there passion and emotion? What needs to be improved, practiced, or removed from the "musical score"?

5. Attend a symphony either online or if possible, in person. Did you enjoy the collaboration between musicians and conductor? What, if anything, did you observe about their relationship?

Journeys, like artists, are born and not made.
—Lawrence Durrell, British novelist and travel writer

Chapter 8
Persevering the Long Journey

I've been following the petite blonde woman with the large backpack for a few hours on the temperamental trail that goes through the rugged mountains of California and Oregon. As we trudge along, the dusty smell of sage and the sweet scent of pine are invigorating. I hear the happy trilling of frogs as we cross a swampy meadow. The crisp morning air turns hot toward midday. I watch as she leans her backpack against a large gray rock in the shade of a gigantic Ponderosa pine. She wipes the sweat from her forehead with a red bandana and gulps down a bottle of water. I pause too, turning my face into the soft breeze as it sifts through the long, fan-like pine branches. The warm air lifts and lowers the evergreen boughs like a wave of encouragement to keep hiking the dirt path.

As if on cue from the beckoning mountain summits ahead, the woman readjusts her backpack and continues walking with a slight limp. Step by step the miles gather behind us. We struggle under the weight of our packs as the ascent gets steeper. We gingerly navigate the unexpected rock piles scattered along the trail. At one point, the path disappears under a long stretch of tree debris and overgrown grass. She pulls out a map and a compass, trying to pinpoint where we are on God's green earth.

I scan the horizon, looking for a familiar landmark—a mountain peak, a lake, or a campground.

She glances down at the shiny gold compass in her hand and begins walking purposefully toward the next set of foothills. I assume she has rediscovered the trail. I eagerly follow along, matching her double-time cadence. Tall green grass whips my thighs as I glance around trying to detect the trail. It's not there. For most of the afternoon, we walk on, without a trail, guided only by a small compass and intuition.

Finally, at the end of the day, the blonde hiker sits at the edge of a lake. She winces as she pulls off her socks and I now understand why she limps. Her toes are like red cherry tomatoes. Blisters pop up at various places on her feet from rubbing the inside of her hiking boots. She dunks her feet in the lake. She lets out a groan as she winces. I assume the glacier fed water numbs her sore feet giving her relief from the pain. After a few minutes, she stands, with hands on her hips, and surveys the beauty of the wild terrain.

I watch and wonder: *Will she make it through another day? What trails will challenge and reshape her character? Will she make it to the end of her journey?*

I turn the page of the book I'm holding to start the next chapter. I reach for the cup of water sitting on the coffee table in my living room in Wyoming and sip the cool liquid. My eyes focus on the words written by the author, but my mind is transported to the Pacific Crest Trail. While my body reclines on the leather couch in my living room, I travel the eleven hundred miles with the author. It took her over three months. I did it in seven days. And my feet didn't suffer a bit!

Walking the path with Cheryl Strayed, author of *Wild: From Lost to Found on the Pacific Crest Trail,* I compared her adventure to the journey of any artist. Strayed carefully prepared and followed the PCT map, yet she dealt with unexpected washed-out trails, fickle weather and a charging bear. Like Strayed's adventure, the details of the artist's trail can't be minutely mapped out. The journey is approximate, not exact. We may have a vague mental understanding of the challenges to become a successful artist, but the reality is completely different.

We've heard about the rigorous climb up the steep mountain of fame. As we begin our creative quest in the foothills and gaze at the elevation of the road to success over the top, we are overcome by the difficulty of the trail. We assume our creative journey is as risky as hiking in the snowy high country. But when we arrive at the lip of a glossy snowfield, we're acutely aware of the danger of sliding to our death. We discover the only way to continue to our destination is to detour around rugged rocky hills. Impatient and disoriented by the change of plans, we unhappily trudge the additional distance on the alternate route.

On the artist path, we expect challenges such as crawling around obstacles like immovable boulders. But we may not anticipate the sudden disappearance of the trail. Because, at times, the path fades, we feel lost and unsure of our next step. We may want to quit the journey, concluding that the road is less traveled because it actually goes nowhere!

During the "wilderness years," as I often called the segment of time after being a creative director, I tried to map out the next segment of my artistic journey. I felt my creative life was on a back-road detour. It seemed my internal compass had led me astray. I wrestled with applying for another creative director position and going back to a familiar routine. I struggled to locate a new trail in a wild attempt to continue the next segment of the artist's pilgrimage. A conversation with a fellow artist, who had navigated the ups and downs of her artist's journey gave me encouragement.

Keep Moving Forward

"I considered my options. There were only two and they were essentially the same. I could go back in the direction I had come

from, or I could go forward in the direction I intended to go."
— Cheryl Strayed, *Wild: From Lost to Found on the Pacific Crest Trail*

"I thought I might be a journalist," states author Amanda Cabot. She sits across from me at a Barnes and Noble Bookstore Café. A slender woman, Amanda wears a Kelly-green handknitted sweater she crafted. We're enjoying a cup of tea on a typical windy Wyoming spring day as she reminisces about her path as a storyteller. Since age seven, Amanda dreamed of being an author. By eight years old, Amanda became involved with the school newspaper. When she was in fifth grade, she had written and directed two plays for her class. Her teacher loved Amanda's creativity and scheduled the short dramas to be performed in various classes in the school. And so began Amanda's journey on the artist's trail.

"But I loved the French language too," Amanda continues as she bounces her tea bag in the paper cup of scalding water. "And since *everyone* knows you can't make a living as a writer, my goal was to get a PhD in French and teach at a college."

While waiting for fellowships to open to pursue her PhD, the military drafted Amanda's husband. Needing a job, she found one as a computer programmer. It wasn't what she had planned but Amanda felt it was a great opportunity. While working full-time, she kept writing and finishing novels.

Amanda leans across the small laminate bistro table. "Years later, I was working away in the IT field and remembered I made a goal to sell my first novel by age thirty."

Although her dream had been to write romantic suspense, one evening while watching TV, she saw a Harlequin Romance advertisement. "I had never read a Harlequin Romance book, but after reading a couple, I realized that it made sense to start with pure romance, and then add suspense later."

She penned a romance novel set in France where she lived as a college student. Although Amanda wasn't even sure how to compose a query letter, she started her note with, "Dear Editor," rather than researching the specific editor's name, and submitted her work to Harlequin.

They promptly rejected it. But her second query was more successful. One week before Amanda's thirtieth birthday, an editor offered a contract for her book.

With her first book published, Amanda composed her next novel, and hoped the contract would come easier and faster. That wasn't to be.

The market changed, editors changed, and the publishing house phased out the line that included her first book. All this contributed to the failure of getting her next work published. Her writing path had faded.

"After getting all the rejection letters, I stopped writing. It wasn't worth the pain,"

Amanda confesses as she fingers the edge of her paper napkin. "But this lasted for a few months. Then I felt a hole, something was missing, and went back to writing."

Sipping my caramel latte, I empathize with Amanda's artistic frustration. Regret bubbled up from leaving the creative director position. I should have bravely stood against the new leader's dysfunction and fought for the artists I cared for. This trail of thought takes me to a murky pool of stench. I remember what is vital to my sanity and self-respect. I left to protect my well-being. I couldn't go back. I had to go forward.

Even though my artist's path vanished, I explored possibilities all the while doing a mundane job to pay the bills. My family wanted chicken noodle casseroles, skinny blue jeans, black tennis shoes, and soft toilet paper. They needed glasses for their eyes, braces for their teeth, and medical check-ups for their health. Although I didn't plan the non-artistic job in the uncreative office, it paid for my family's essentials. It was the detour I navigated for the welfare of my kids.

Five years after leaving the creative director position, and while navigating in the gray cubicles of work life, I decided to pursue a master's degree. It was a two-year, online program in

Communication and Leadership. Since I couldn't find a job in the creative field, an education would allow me to trade the money counting for teaching and inspiring others. For 942 days, I read textbooks and scholarly articles. And then I wrote class discussion posts and research papers (which I approached as an author writing a novel—I couldn't help it!).

In the beginning, the professors corrected my grammar and phrasing. Grammar Girl became my new BFF. After the first year, nearly every instructor commented how they enjoyed my writing style.

During this time, when my nights and weekends focused on schoolwork, I didn't feel like an artist. My writing was about communication theory, not people's stories. My mind focused on critical thinking and not creativity.

While walking forward, I swung between panic and hope. I felt panicked, searching for a sign to guide me out of the bewildering feelings of being lost. I hoped that somehow the master's degree would reveal a new path to a job.

Explore While Lost

"There are several ways to react to being lost. One is to panic: this was usually Valentina's first impulse. Another is to abandon yourself to lostness, to allow the fact that you've misplaced yourself to change the way you experience the world."
— Audrey Niffenegger, *Her Fearful Symmetry*

While Amanda wrote novels and received rejection letters, she explored other writing opportunities. The technical magazines she read focused on programmers who developed new systems but ignored those who were responsible for maintaining and upgrading those systems. Seeing the need, Amanda typed up articles to equip and motivate her fellow programmers. She became an editor for an information technology magazine and ended up composing four books for IT professionals. She admitted, "I did it to add to my resume, but I enjoyed it and got paid for most of it."

As Amanda wrote for work, she also wrote for hire. Amanda was paid a flat fee for five of her stories, but wasn't credited, and didn't receive royalties for her creativity. Two of those books involved turning two soap opera scripts into a book for one publisher. This learning opportunity caused her to master writing a cliffhanger at the end of each chapter.

She wrote three books about a teenage sleuth for three different editors. It was a lesson in working hard for the money and dealing with one horrible editor. Amanda still wrote a book a year and still received rejection letters. During this time, she felt like she was always juggling the job and writing. And she acquired another lesson: She could write whenever and wherever.

"I found I was content writing for both the IT magazine and the fiction market. I would have continued except I found where I was supposed to be." Amanda attended a writer's conference where a speaker asked, "Is writing what you do or who you are?" The answer to this question is critical for any writer or aspiring author. Amanda found she couldn't stop writing. "It's who I am!" Amanda triumphantly professes.

I wasn't as content in my lost state. Even after completing a master's degree, the path didn't become clear. As a former leader of artists who encouraged others' creative direction, figuring out where *I* should be going was one of the most difficult segments on my artist journey.

The realization of being lost on the artist's trail challenged my every preconceived idea about my creative road map. When disorientated on the artist journey I wanted to cling to what I always knew, stick to the familiar trail. But I couldn't go back to writing dramas, creating videos, or leading artists. The way I approached creativity as a leader was in the past. Going forward and looking for the artist's road meant wrestling with identity and creativity. I thought I needed to travel a single narrow path of writer workshops, agents, and publishing. You may have a similar plan: *I'll only do oil paintings, major art shows, and then arrive on the New York art scene. I don't want to learn hip-hop dance. There is no way I'm going to direct or write a script. I feel insecure to sing different musical styles.* Often this thinking limits our capabilities until we *have to* adapt to the terrain in front of us.

Granted, we need to be aware of our creative strengths and weaknesses. But we may be constricting ourselves by a narrow artist description or path to success. When we're bewildered by the overgrowth of the one-way trail, we move from lost to found by an inner tug-of-war of letting go of the backpack of rocks that weighs us down. It could be artistic traits, or negative friends, or simple insecurity, or even an error in goals.

We have to wrestle with our preconceived ideas of success. What would success look like for me as an artist? Will mimicking other artists help us find our voice, unveil our creative uniqueness? If we contend with the lost trail, if we don't panic, we can allow the disorientation to force us to look for new roads.

Our human nature resists adjusting or growing. It's why the high school quarterback stays in his hometown and lives in retrospect of his glory days. It's why, still today, we see the mullet or Farrah Fawcett hairstyles! We grasp with a tight fist onto a perception which doesn't serve us well for a better future. It slows the transformation of our potential success.

In fact, it's our confusion which prompts us to explore paths we once ignored or shunned. It's at this moment of being lost that we are on the precipice of a new discovery. In desperation and fear of creative death, we move forward to save our artistic selves. Our gutsiness to step ahead makes us more alert to the unexpected. Amanda discovered that not only could she write fiction, but she could write technical books for the IT professionals. As we meander along looking for a clear path, we are actually forging a new trail that will widen our perspective as artists.

Be Open to the Unexpected Path

"Adventure is allowing the unexpected to happen to you. Exploration is experiencing what you have not experienced before. How can there be any adventure, any exploration, if you let somebody else—above all, a travel bureau—arrange everything before-hand?"
— Richard Aldington, *Death of a Hero*

Amanda retired from her day job, and she and her husband moved to Cheyenne, Wyoming. They had visited the small western town a number of times and liked the friendliness of the locals. One month after unpacking the moving boxes, Amanda received a call from a close friend who had been her roommate in France. Amanda's friend revealed she was dying of leukemia.

Throughout her friend's illness, Amanda kept in constant contact and listened to her grieve over leaving her children behind. Even though Amanda's friend was heartbroken about missing her children's marriages and holding her unborn grandchildren, she looked forward to heaven.

Amanda paused, memories filled her eyes with tears. "I can't believe she's been gone thirteen years. She gave me a beautiful piece of French porcelain, but it's her belief in God's love for people that I most treasure."

Walking this passageway with her friend was a turning point for Amanda's writing career. A few years earlier, while in Texas doing a workshop, someone suggested to Amanda that she should write for the Christian market. Amanda wasn't interested. She felt the genre could be too preachy.

Because of the impact of her friend's life and death, Amanda decided to read a few Christian authors and explored the publishing possibilities. She found another agent and began writing with a renewed purpose. Her first book published for the Christian market was *Paper Roses*. In this book, the minister gives a lengthy sermon. Amanda softly chuckles. "My favorite review of the book stated they loved Cabot's non-preachy style!"

Confidence emanates from the blonde artist like an expensive French perfume. Amanda now has twenty-two inspirational novels and novellas in addition to more than twenty books she wrote for the secular market. And she enjoys working with the Christian publishers. Through her exploration and openness to the unexpected along the artist's journey, Amanda has found her creative place.

I was looking for my creative place when the unexpected happened. I had a garage sale in which I tried to sell my children's desks. They were a drab brown and no one looked twice at them. At a friend's suggestion, I used white paint to cover the drab brown and added a black chevron design to the top of the desk. Then I posted the two refinished desks on a few Facebook yard sale sites. They sold within twenty minutes!

I took the $250 profit, bought a few more drab desks and colorful paint, and sold them. I repeated the processes of painting and selling furniture for a few months while I applied for jobs with the local government and college. I wrote a resume and painted a desk. I interviewed for a state trainer position and painted a dresser. Finally, with no legitimate job, I created a Facebook page, called Broken to Beauty, to market the painted furniture I created. I didn't know what I was doing, I just kept marching forward. I painted end tables, desks, lamps, chairs, and bedframes. I added painted daisies, lilies, birds in cages, and birds liberated from cages.

Two years into this adventure, a friend told me, "I slap on paint, but you apply it with an artist's touch."

"I do?" I didn't comprehend what she noticed about my hobby turned business.

I happened upon a Facebook group for people painting and selling furniture. An interior designer from Chicago created the page to help painters, like myself, to stage and sell furniture. I joined the group and soon heard them identify themselves as furniture artists. That label resonated with me.

When sales of my furniture were slow, I wondered if I should quit. I questioned if my pieces were trendy and whether they appealed to consumers. But then, I'd have a couple of sales and talk to the buyer who was over-the-moon with my creation.

I'm still very much at the beginning of my artist's journey. I've only consciously walked the artist's path for the few years I've painted furniture. The writing career path is still a mystery to be solved. And I work full-time as a corporate trainer. I haven't spent twenty-five years persevering for the mere love of writing like Amanda.

Redefine Your Artistic Success

"...there ain't no journey what don't change you some..."
—David Mitchell, *Cloud Atlas*

"Never give up," Amanda advises other artists. "You may have to adapt and change, but persevere and keep learning." Through the rejection letters, the nasty editors or the inconvenient writing times, Amanda endured. From the publishing of her first novel to present day, Amanda learned from her artist's trail, adjusting and maturing her writing style.

In Amanda's book *Scattered Petals*, a young woman is raped and her personal healing process dominates the narrative. Amanda admits it was the most difficult storyline to write. After the book released, emails from readers swamped her inbox. They made Amanda cry and yet smile at the same time. For Amanda, success in her writing career isn't decided by the amount of her royalty check but in delivering a message through her writing that helps people through tough times.

Amanda sips her Earl Gray tea and sits the near empty white cup on the brown laminate table. "Nothing compares to knowing my stories change people's lives."

My art may not have as dramatic effect on a person as Amanda's writing has. Nor will my furniture be featured in *House Beautiful* or *Country Living*. But that's not my goal or my definition of artistic success.

I sold a dresser to a single mom and delivered it to her home. Later, she texted images of her new dresser nestled in a corner of her sparse bedroom. She had placed her few trinkets on top, snapped a picture, and wrote, "I love your work—it makes my room so beautiful." Creating beauty from worn and broken furniture that gives joy to others is my definition of success.

Success as an artist in the local community has to be redefined as something other than the typical Hollywood ending of fame and money. I hope with all my heart that if you dream of receiving an Oscar, or a Grammy, or a Pulitzer Prize, you will persevere until that moment is realized.

But...

The success of an artist's journey can be defined in many ways. Not just by a twenty-four-karat, gold-plated, eight-and-a-half-pound statuette on a shelf. Chasing an award may give us focus and motivation. It will challenge us to unearth the very best of our creativity. But it may also make us blind to the landmarks of achievement along the trail.

What if success is defined by the growth of the artist and the impact of local community? What if finishing an eighty-thousand-word novel is celebrated as an artistic win? What if auditioning, for the first time, as an extra for the community theater is a personal triumph? Can an artist claim success if she is a local favorite who performs on her guitar at a popular coffee house? Should a trophy be given to an artist who starts a dance company in a cowboy town?

On the artist's journey, we will have moments where we look over our shoulder and realize how far we've come. The realization we could have quit the trail, pitched a tent, and become bear bait, but didn't, should define our success as artists.

Learning a new artistic skill, exploring an avant-garde perspective, or completing an artistic goal, are moments of success. At these places on our creative path, we must build a cairn, a landmark commemorating our achievements.

Ancient civilizations built cairns, a stack of rocks, to mark a significant place for their people. Cairns can be seen on a hill where a successful battle was fought. Hunters would pile rocks to identify a special passage through an area.

We artists must identify our own artistic advances and build our own landmarks where we can visit from time to time to celebrate and remember the joy of this journey. We can't wait for others to recognize our points of success and hand us a shiny gold statue.

It might be a long wait.

It might never happen.

But an artist who defines and celebrates their own successes won't need that one huge statue, for we will have collected our own cairns of success long before.

Accept the Risks of the Artist Journey

"To travel is worth any cost or sacrifice,"
—Elizabeth Gilbert, *Eat, Pray, Love*

As I approach the start of a trail in Rocky Mountain National Park, I notice a faded sheet of paper on a weathered signpost. I step in closer to read the barely legible type. It's a list warning hikers about the possible dangers encountered on the trail, such as wild animals, falling rocks or trees, and a gastrointestinal sickness from drinking stream water. I pat my full container of filtered water and tuck my protein bar in the side pocket of the daypack saddled on my back.

The list further warns of changing weather, lightning, snowfields, flooding streams, and hypothermia. I tilt my head upward to the cornflower blue sky void of clouds. It looks peaceful now, but I remembered climbing near Vail, Colorado, and hiding under the overhang of a rock wall as fingers of lightning zapped their power around me. Yes, I need to be aware of the weather, and animals, and rocks, and snowfields.

While the list of warnings was lengthy and intimidating, I also knew to hike this trail would promise a view of uncommon beauty not seen at the lower elevation. I looked forward to discovering something new on the trail. Maybe it would be a wildflower, or a small friendly animal. I could discover a waterfall from a snow-field, or rainbow trout gliding below the surface of a mountain lake. Perhaps I would encounter one of the dangers of the trail, but I hoped I could overcome it, reach the end of the path, and enjoy all the trek would give me.

The artist's journey will have moments of danger. When re-spected and navigated with savvy, dangerous is good. It requires us to problem solve. It demands adjustments of our habits and usual creative processes. I could warn you about sudden per-sonal hailstorms and the disappearance of the artist trail. I'm sure Amanda would warn you about the unsteadying effects of rejection and the terror of certain editors. But those dangers may not apply to your journey. It's important to prepare yourself for the trip, to consider the cost of taking the trail, but potential danger shouldn't keep us from proceeding along the artist's way.

As you will find, there is no exact route for your journey—it will unfold in ways that are unique to you, your gifts, and your level of perseverance and stamina. However, I'm confident your journey will reveal itself by continuing to move forward, explor-ing while lost, be open to the unexpected path, redefining suc-cess and accepting the risk factor of creativity.

I wish I would have recognized the artist within at age fifteen rather than forty. And yet my journey happened the way it was supposed to. Amanda Cabot's artist path unfolded the way it was supposed to. Your journey will have circumstances and ex-periences that will be totally different than mine or any of the artists in this book.

But our connection will be our stories of exploration along the creative path and finding our creative place.

Our commonality will be the unexpected detours that have transformed us into the best artists we can be.

And our journey will be alike in that we dared to be brave and persevered as artists in a world that needs us.

Sit and rest from your busyness to contemplate these questions about your artist's journey.

Map Key

1. What steps are needed to go forward on your creative path?
2. Do you feel lost on your artist's journey?
3. What artistic adventure needs exploring?
4. Create a definition of success for your artist's journey.
5. Take time to look at what you've accomplished as an artist. Build a cairn to mark those significant moments of creative achievement.
6. Buy a travel book for a new destination and explore a new place.
7. Paint rocks and write inspirational quotes on them to display near your creative space.

Not everyone can be a great artist, but a great artist can come from anywhere.
—Anton Ego from the film *Ratatouille*

Chapter 9
Every Stage Needs a Backdrop

My fingertips press against the cool, golden yellow walls hoping to conjure up the images of all the actors who have performed in this Broadway theater. Closing my eyes, I lean forward until my warm forehead presses against the cold plaster. I envision a cluster of chatty, nervous actors as they audition for roles. I hear echoes of triumphant shouts by happy actors who got callbacks. The anguishing echoes from those who don't get chosen ring a little longer. I imagine an artist standing outside the audition room, so consumed with fear, she forgoes the tryout and walks away.

"We're going to go to the back door of the theater to see Daniel."

The voice of my sixteen-year-old daughter, Lauren, snaps my head back from the theater wall and to reality. It's our last day in New York City, and Lauren, her friend Liz and I had just experienced the show, *How to Succeed in Business Without Really Trying*, starring Daniel Radcliffe and John Larroquette. For a Wyoming girl, it's a bucket-list occasion. The magic of Broadway didn't disappoint as Harry Potter sang and danced in a business suit, and Larroquette improvised his lines with the flair of a court jester.

I gaze back through the theater door at the glowing stage lights reluctant to leave this experience. With a sigh of satisfaction and a smile in my soul, I turn and float out the front door and onto the sidewalk, glancing left, then right, trying to catch a glimpse of my daughter and her friend.

"Ya must be waiting for someone to get an autograph from Daniel Radcliffe," states a man with a Long Island accent. "My wife and girls are over there too. I don't see what all the screaming is about." He chuckles.

We are standing in front of the theater under the glow of the Broadway lights, and look over at the mob of girls waiting by the back exit.

"Yeah, my daughter and her friend are over there hyperventilating over that cute boy with the British accent." As soon as I speak, he squints at me and asks, "Where ya from?"

"Wyoming."

I pause, trying to gauge his response to one of the most unrecognizable western states.

"It's the state right above Colorado," I explain to him, as I've had to respond to this question several times since arriving in New York City four days ago.

"Oh, yeah. I know where it is. Always wanted to go out West." He shifts his glance from my eyes to the top of my head as if he's wondering why I'm not wearing a cowboy hat.

"First time to a Broadway show?"

How did he guess? Self-conscious of my old black trench coat and worn running shoes, I look at the ground and kick at a cigarette butt.

"Yeah, first time, and the show was absolutely glorious. I've never seen anything like the elaborate sets rolling on and off the stage."

The man points down the street toward the east. "I live on Long Island. It's an easy train ride into the city. We catch a play, or go to a museum, or shop. Then it's an easy train ride out of the busy city to our quiet home."

"Wow, that's amazing," I reply wistfully. "I would love to be able to live close enough to do that. This Wyoming girl learned a few tricks such as figuring out how to navigate the train systems, catching a cab, and now standing on Broadway."

"So what kind of cultural experiences do you have in Wyoming? Cowboy ballets?" A small chuckle accidently escapes and he quickly convers his mouth with his hand.

"Maybe you have gunshot art out West?" The small chuckle opens the gate to full shoulder bouncing and nostril-snorting laughter. His mischievous dark eyes tell me he's teasing.

It must be difficult for a person from Long Island who has easy access to the best art in the world to picture the art community in Wyoming. No, Cheyenne doesn't have a Museum of Modern Art, a cluster of Broadway theaters, or the high-kicking Rockettes.

"He talked to us!"

My daughter and her friend bounce toward us.

"He said," Lauren mimics a British accent, "It's your birthday? Well happy birthday, Lauren!"

The Long Island man waves at me and wanders over toward the excited crowd waiting at the theater's back exit.

"Nice meeting you," I shout to the man.

I turn to Lauren and Liz, trying to make sense of what they said. "But it's not your birthday—" I stammer. A mother never forgets the ten torturous hours of labor, so I know her birthday isn't in October.

"I know but..." my daughter looks at Liz and giggles.

Liz explains, "We told Daniel it was her birthday hoping he'd stop and talk to us." She looks at Lauren. "And it worked! We have the video on our phones." She opens her phone and I watch their interaction with Harry Potter as he sweetly wishes Lauren a happy birthday.

Looking up from their extraordinary Broadway moment, I

catch the eye of the man from Long Island. He is surrounded by a woman and two preteen girls who I presume are his family. As Lauren, Liz, and I move around the sidewalk to pass them, hands are flapping, and voices are accelerating as all three ladies also recount their meeting with Radcliffe. The evening curtain is dropping on the day as we stroll down the street illuminated by Broadway marquee lights.

"While Daniel Radcliffe was singing to your fake birthday," I smile at both girls, "I talked with a man who lives on Long Island and catches a lot of Broadway shows. I can't even imagine what it would be like to live close enough to see the best actors in the world."

"Or catch a concert at Central Park," Lauren states.

"Or attend Fashion Week," adds Liz.

"Maybe someday we'll experience more of the art scene of New York City," I glance over my shoulder and see Radcliffe sprint to a waiting black vehicle, jump through the open car door, and drive off into the sunset.

Why This Backdrop?

Days later, after arriving back in Wyoming, discouragement clings to my creative soul like white doghair on a black sweater. *What's the point of being an artist in a small town?*

The trip helped me understand why artists migrate to the Big Apple. What artist isn't inspired by the city's lush creative scenery of music, theater, dance, and fine art.

Twenty-seven years ago, when I unexpectedly landed in the windy city of Cheyenne, Wyoming, it should have been the last place to write an artist's narrative. But it's where unruly gusts rustled the pages of my life like dust in a cyclone. What seemed like chaotic flying debris was more a removal of untethered conjecture of what I should be or how I should act. It twisted and blew apart the leaflets of my life exposing a story of creativity.

The unlikely destination didn't hinder my artist's path, but became the backdrop, the setting, for my creative journey. I have witnessed this Wild West scene evolve as I added unique details to the Cheyenne backdrop.

History is engraved with artists who influenced and changed their communities. Georgia O'Keeffe, a Wisconsin native, broke the rules of realism for pure abstraction and changed not only the art culture of the region but the international art world. Harriet Beecher Stowe's story of *Uncle Tom's Cabin* confronted the philosophy of people as property, which instigated hysteria in Ohio, and eventually influenced President Lincoln. Illinois native Michael Jackson broke down racial barriers with his music video, *Billie Jean*. His music and dance moves changed pop culture. These artists, and many more, transformed the culture of the world, but the change began first with the artist, then the neighborhood they lived in.

Some creative people reside in a rural area by choice. They are drawn to the climate, inspired by the landscape, or spellbound by the one flashing *Bar & Grill* sign. They are content, even creatively exhilarated, by an out-of-the-way town.

"I fell in love with Wyoming. The sagebrush prairie spoke to me," author Amanda Cabot explains. "After living on the east coast, I wanted the 233 days of sunshine, the clean air, and low humidity. I love the blue sky with the puffy cumulus clouds. And the Rocky Mountains are close by. Plus, Cheyenne has friendly people. It's a good place to live."

Leah Beauchamp came to Cheyenne because both her parents and her husband's parents lived there. Dan Holroyd grew up in Cheyenne and graduated from the same high school where he presently teaches. Shane Ingram arrived in Cheyenne from Casper, Wyoming, as he looked for a friendly place to open his tattoo shop.

But some artists end up in a community by circumstance. Their family, job, or schooling brought them to an unfamiliar city and region. Such was the case for Jonathan Hedger. The military relocated his family to Warren Air Force Base, and he ended up staying in Cheyenne.

A change in employment brought me to Cheyenne. Soon after arriving, it became apparent the common pastime is complaining about the wind or lack of things to do.

The Easy Role of a Critic

At first glance, Cheyenne is an absurd setting for artistic inspiration. This small town has a few museums depicting the Old West, an artist's guild, two small theaters, and floozy-strutting saloon girls in the melodrama during Frontier Days.

Imagine what a Broadway critic would write concerning Cheyenne's art culture:

Though sunny, Cheyenne experiences extreme wind, cold, heat, hail, and wind (yes it deserves to be mentioned again because of its fierceness) sure to discourage any artists seeking a paradise. The town is isolated from metropolitan areas like Denver, Colorado, which is 100 miles to the south, or New York City, which is 1742.8 miles to the east. Therefore, the backdrop is simple, with an element of wilderness. I give it a thumbs down.

As for the actor's costumes: faded black skinny jeans with Van skater kicks contrast the blue, worn Wranglers with brown leather Ariat boots. I give it a thumbs up for variety. To review the overall performance of artists, there lacks the elegance and flair of Broadway...thumbs down.

But what a Broadway critic misses at first glance is the organic growth of Cheyenne's art scene. The Civic Center contracts eighty nationally known shows a year. A monthly Art Walk encourages locals to visit businesses which display work by community artists. There is the Symphony, Ballet Wyoming, and the Chamber Singers. There are quality art shows at Edge Fest, popular bands at Fridays on the Plaza, and critically acclaimed plays at the Little

Theater. A critic might miss these artistic endeavors, just like a critic missed the creativity of a rat.

In the movie, *Ratatouille*, Anton Ego, the food critic, writes:

"In many ways, the work of a critic is easy. We risk very little yet enjoy a position over those who offer up their work and their selves to our judgment. We thrive on negative criticism, which is fun to write and to read. But the bitter truth we critics must face is that in the grand scheme of things, the average piece of junk is probably more meaningful than our criticism designating it so. But there are times when a critic truly risks something, and that is in the discovery and the defense of the new."

Yeah, it's easy to give a negative review of a modest city's artistic setting. Anyone can become the town critic—it creates the illusion of superiority to other artists. *I must point out the truth of what's wrong because no one else sees it, because, well, I'm smarter than everyone else.*

Arrogance and negativity separate the critic from the community of artists and don't help the city. I tire of the critics who stand on the edge of town and throws eggs at those working to better the place.

I believe critics pester with their unfavorable assessments as a distraction from their own lack of artistic initiative and growth. It takes less energy to criticize than to create imaginative and unique art. An artist's pessimistic view only hinders their journey, and, in the end, the critic's role is just a bit part.

Open Casting Call for Creative Roles

So here you are. You live in a neighborhood, a suburb, a parish, a town, or a city. You have a backdrop and now you must discover the creative roles to play. All have impact to your locality. All prove the destination doesn't dictate the quality or success of your journey. And you get to choose.

It may be a classical role where the artist is attracted to what "speaks to them" and allows the audience to glean their own interpretations. Many artists love playing this part. The artist explores his or her own experience and creates out of that emotion or thought. In Chapter 5, Leah mentioned using her sadness over a miscarriage to inspire her dance. An audience member came up after the performance and told Leah how it touched her soul. While the dance spoke to Leah and allowed her to channel her pain and frustration, the observer felt Leah's emotion and interpreted into her own life. The classical role can be risky in that some observers may not understand the artist's expression. The person may walk away from the art encounter unaffected and unchanged. But that might be one person in a larger number which still remembers the dance, the painting, the sculpture, the song, or the play that left them altered with a new perspective.

Some artists choose the role of a servant. This artist creates art according to what others want and will pay for. For centuries, this was the common role of an artist. Portrait painters were commissioned to create images of kings, queens, and other elites. Musicians were responsible to compose operas and symphonies for religious holidays. In Chapter 2, the tattoo artist illustrates this role. He draws on skin according to the image chosen by a customer. He may add his expertise, but if a client wants a bird, he creates a bird.

While meeting a need in their city is important, it can be frustrating for the artist who wants to express themselves beyond the consumer's tastes and preferences. For instance, Western art is popular in Cheyenne, and many creatives go with this genre. It sells well to both the local and visiting consumer. But for those artists who don't create Western art, sales can be challenging. Either they find their own unique niche and provide variety to the town, like a tattoo artist, or they expand their market beyond the city's walls.

A third role for the artist is one with innovative and progressive ideas—a modernist. They gravitate toward new ideas and new expressions of art. The creative who plays this part isn't satisfied with tradition but pushes boundaries and explores contemporary concepts. Modernist artists experiment with color, materials and form. While this role is usually associated with painters, it can include any artist who seeks cutting-edge creativity. It might be an author who experiments with literary form and expression. A musician may use new approaches to harmony and rhythm. In my opinion, composer Lin-Manuel Miranda plays the role of modernist. He uses the contemporary style of rap with traditional theater in the Broadway musical *Hamilton*.

Because many people resist change, the modernist artist risks being misunderstood and criticized. It may take a while for the innovative and uncommon art to be accepted. But it is the modernist artists like painters van Gogh and Picasso, or musicians Johann Strauss and The Beach Boys, who have influenced change in the art world.

Lastly, there is the global artist who markets his or her art but with a broad interest and variety that appeals to many outside their city. This role isn't limited by the size of the town or region. With the use of social media and online markets, they can interact with and market to anyone.

The artist in this role expands the edges of the small-town backdrop to that of the world neighborhood. And in many ways all artists in today's world can be a global artist. Authors are now self-publishing and selling their ebooks on Amazon. Painters and photographers sell their art on Etsy or through their personal websites. An artist's audience is no longer contained by the city's boundaries.

We gravitate toward one or two roles which are comfortable with. But there is one role that all artists can play. And dare I say, *must* play.

The One Role You Must Play

While there are different roles to be played in a local community that are each uniquely important, the most significant role for an artist is an investor! This part is played by an artist who assesses the needs of the people in that area, inspires a cast of artists on the local stage and influences the outcome of the show!

When I worked for a nonprofit organization, the brainstorming group of artists (we called ourselves "The Dream Team") searched for a way to creatively influence our city. We heard about the challenge of parents of children with disabilities to find child care for a date night. The average babysitter isn't equipped to watch a child with disabilities. So, we decided to host a Friday night event at the Community Building for the kids to paint, play games, or dance while the parents went to dinner and a movie.

At the end of the three-hour evening, I was surprised at the responses by parents and artists alike.

"I can't believe you would watch our child so that we reconnect with each other," gushed a mom as we watched her son dab a paintbrush into red paint.

"Thank you for watching my son," said a dad as he gathered his son to leave at the end of the art night. "It was pretty gutsy for you artists to entertain our kids with art."

One Dream team artist confided, "I was skeptical about interacting with special needs children, but I enjoyed helping them paint. And it felt so good to help families in our community."

The role of investor is a visionary for the lasting power of art on the social setting of the area. The artist who plays this part is available to share their expertise and wisdom by teaching or coaching others. They mentor kids and young adults, shaping the next generation of creatives. They invite non-artists to experience emotional and mental refreshment through creative activities. While this artist identifies with one of the roles previously discussed, such as classical, modernist, servant, etc., it's through the capacity of an investor where they find the greatest success.

During our long and challenging journey as artists, we focus on perfecting the artist's role or roles we've chosen. We spend the time and effort to reach our potential. However, at some point, we aren't just playing a role but become a role model. Someone is watching us and shaping their own artistic future. From our example, a young artist will commit to the artist's journey and choose a creative role. Being a role model can happen unknowingly and haphazardly. Or we can mentor other artists purposely and intentionally.

I admit it. I have intentionally mentored others in leadership and life issues but not artistically. My creative influence has been haphazard and sporadic. During my time as creative director, it wasn't on my mind to mentor others. My way of playing the investor role was to give artists opportunities and encouragement. And I was an artist newbie too. I had just started my own artist's journey. So my experience with deliberately mentoring artists is limited. Until now.

Back in Chapter 2, I discussed the role of mentors and how I lacked a personal creative advisor. So I searched for my mentors in books. It was in writing where an author guided me in the artist's way. It is in my writing where I purposely and intentionally endeavor to advise, guide, and coach you the reader. While being aware of your impact on those observing your artist's journey, it's best to mentor on purpose.

As we come alongside this artist newbie, we create a legacy which will most likely outlive any art we make. This investor in people role will produce an internal satisfaction which doesn't tarnish or fade. It can't be judged for artistic skill, technique, or beauty. In the end, this Oscar-worthy role will define you, but it will come at a cost.

The role of an investor will challenge your time, energy, and ego. It takes a few hours to teach or mentor. And that time will be spent away from your writing, painting, dancing, gardening, or composing music. You may not get your art project done on schedule. However, time invested in others has a way of coming back at you. The mentor relationships will enrich your well-being.

The investor role will take energy. As we pour into another, our physical strength may lessen. Our emotions may drain as we encourage and have difficult conversations. We may feel disappointed that our mentee didn't listen to our advice and made poor decisions. Relationships take energy but they can also inspire us by their creative curiosity and growth.

Investing time and energy in future artists will affect our ego. It may also humble us when we see our mentee surpassing our own skills. We might have to deal with personal jealousy and insecurities. Or our ego may bruise when the mentee doesn't soar as we anticipated. And we'll have to remind ourselves of personal boundaries and living vicariously through another. But if you have the courage to overcome these challenges, the role of investor will give you another sort of creative satisfaction and success. It's the role of investor where the artist ultimately comes to thrive in the local community.

"Wyoming is about hard work. Many people here don't have time for beauty." Leah explains. "Ballet Wyoming Dance Company wants to embrace the locals and add value to their lives outside the normal rural box." Leah adds, "I want to bring an escape, or a joy, and offer a message from my dancer spirit to their spirit."

Dan, a high school music teacher, advises young musicians is to not focus on one thing but be prepared to do a variety of things. "I challenge young musicians to take song writing classes, write their own music, and to study the business side of being a professional musician. I encourage artists to study marketing and be able to effectively promote themselves both in Cheyenne, and globally," he explains.

Dan is involved in a volunteer band which plays at the Civic Center or at local parks. "Playing for your own enjoyment and the betterment of the local community can be defined as success," Dan concludes.

Jonathan teaches dance classes in Cheyenne. He loves sharing his passion for dance with others. "I really enjoy watching them grow as artists," says Jonathan. He teaches dance after work. And after his rehearsals with Ballet Wyoming Dance Company. He works a regular eight-to-five, forty-hour-a-week desk job with two weeks paid vacation. He doesn't get paid to dance. "In a small rural community, dancing with the ballet company is a labor of love."

Jonathan is reimbursed for his investor role in Cheyenne by engaging with the next generation and watching them grow as artists. Jonathan doesn't aspire for a big stage in New York or any large metropolis. "I wouldn't turn down an opportunity," Jonathan says with a smile, "but I'm happy to perform in Cheyenne and further the cultural maturity in the area."

As I moved toward my passion for creativity, I became aware of the role of an artist in the community. It didn't matter that I was in rural Cheyenne, Wyoming, an improbable place for someone to find their artist's soul. It doesn't matter if you live in a small town or a modest suburb or a large city. The impactful role the artist plays in the local community proves the destination doesn't have to dictate the quality or success of our artist's journey.

The artist's destination is more than a blue dot on Google Maps. It's the very place where you and I jump into the stage backdrop and explore creative roles which add our splash of artistic spirit to the huge canvas of the region. Throughout our journey, we may adapt to many roles in different seasons. But it will be the role of investor, if you choose, which will cause you to thrive, to succeed, to soar. Isn't that what we hope and plan for?

I'm very cautious to equate success with monetary value. It's too unstable. It's too dependent on critics or the approval of select groups of people. But I can embrace the idea of creative growth and investment as success. I can unwaveringly encourage you to thrive in ways unconnected to money. It's this role of investor, of being mindful of mentoring and creating a legacy which has gripped my heart and soul, that causes me to move forward in my artist's journey and finish this book for you. It is this role which I hope to impact your storyline on the backdrop of the local community.

I encourage you to embrace your backdrop, explore your artistic roles, and build your stage. Trust that your destination has benefits for both you and your community. It's on that community stage, against the unique backdrop of your hometown, where the culmination of an inner journey occurs. You will not only discover your creative part in the region, but also become the best version of artistry possible and leave a legacy for others to follow. And that is the true definition of creative success.

Use these questions to identify your backdrop and role.

Stage Props

1. Are you a critic of your neighborhood? Or an investor in your community?
2. How does the backdrop of your location affect you artistically?
3. What role do you play in your community? Are you satisfied with that script?
4. What's your reaction to the role of investor?
5. How can you invest in the people of your community?
6. What theater production did you last enjoy? Why? How did it connect to your artist's journey?

And in his lifetime, a man will play many parts.
    —Shakespeare

Chapter 10
The Stage

Act 1

SETTING: At center stage is a green room, with a doorway to small stage with three actors and ten seated audience members.

AT RISE: A play is presented on a small stage for an audience from a local community. We listen in to the audience's responses to the play. At the end of the scene, we hear the actor's exchange in the green room. The actors join a cast of artists center stage.

CHARACTORS:

YOUNG BOY
YOUNG GIRL
TEEN GIRL 1
TEEN GIRL 2
MIDDLE-AGED WOMAN
MIDDLE-AGED MAN
FOUR AUDIENCE EXTRAS
NARRATOR
WOMAN

ACTOR/BUSINESSMAN
ACTOR/ROOFER
ACTOR/PATROLMAN
FEMALE DANCER
MALE DANCER
BAND TEACHER
TATTOO ARTIST
AUTHOR
MUSICIAN

(Two rows of ten talkative people of various ages are seated in front of the SMALL STAGE set. Spotlights on the small crowd flash signaling the people to murmur the last of their conversations. After a few seconds, the SMALL STAGE lights fade up to reveal two male actors sitting on an old dusty blue couch. There is a knock and another actor walks through the "front door." The actors on stage mime a conversation.)

YOUNG BOY: *(Pokes a YOUNG GIRL sitting in chair next to him.)* Does this hurt? *(Pokes her again.)* How about this?

YOUNG GIRL: *(Shoves BOY's hand away.)* Stop it! MOM!

ACTOR: Well, now, aren't you something else...Officer FRIENDLY. *(ACTOR puts emphasis on Friendly. The YOUNG BOY turns his attention from poking his little sister to the actors on the stage with his mouth hanging open.)*

TEENGIRL 1: *(To her friend, TEEN GIRL 2, sitting next to her.)* I wish Officer Friendly would have been the one to give me the speeding ticket last week. *(She giggles.)*

(Toward the end of the row, a middle-aged lady leans forward in her seat, and then throws her whole body back in raucous laughter.)

MIDDLE-AGED WOMAN: *(Pokes her husband.)* That is so you!

NARRATOR: *(Standing downstage left. Turns from watching the play on the Small Stage to address the larger audience.)*

The actors on stage memorized their lines during their regular jobs of highway patrolman, roof contractor, and businessman. Though their livelihood demands much of their time and focus, they found space to become a character that mirrored life to the audience.

It didn't take a professional actor to deliver the message. A special trip to a Broadway theater wasn't necessary for a spectator to receive a story about life. All that was needed to make a difference in the life of an onlooker, a community, is the artist's joy of creating, and the heart and courage to share it. *(Turns back to watch the Small Stage.)*

ACTOR: Fair? You want me to be fair? *(Pause)* That's the place where you ride wild horses, wrestle greased pigs, and step in cow manure!

(SMALL STAGE lights fade to black. The crowd laughs and applauds. The actors make their way through the blacked-out backstage into the green room.)

ACTOR/ROOF CONTRACTOR: *(As he grabs the highway patrolman's neck and mischievously grins.)* Remember you'll always be Officer Friendly to me. *(Pauses)* Even if I am speeding at eighty-five miles per hour!

(The ACTOR/PATROLMAN points his first two fingers at his eyes, then at the roofer's.)

ACTOR/BUSINESSMAN: Wow that was fun. The audience really got into it. *(He grabs his rolled-up script left on the table where he had been rehearsing.)*

ACTOR/ROOFER: We did pretty good for a bunch of guys from the sticks. *(The roofer hangs both arms around the other two actors.)*

ACTOR/PATROLMAN: Yeah, but don't give up your day job just yet.

ACTOR/ROOFER: Not until the boss lady gives me an Oscar. *(The ACTOR/ ROOFER winks at the WOMAN and the men walk out of the green room and stand center stage.)*

WOMAN: If you deny your artist's identity, refuse the mission, or quit the artist's journey, your community will fail to experience the laughter, joy, tears, pain, and insight in a dimension that only you offer. You may provide laughter in a comedy play for someone who had a long work week of work. You may comfort through a song performance at a funeral. It could be jewelry you created which is purchased to celebrate a relationship. Maybe it's your book which allows someone to escape the stress of life and invigorates them to carry on. Or you may create a peaceful garden that brings friends together. Grasp your power to influence others through your creativity in your neighborhood. Let's make an artist's pact. *(Artists enter stage left and stand in a loose group, only two people deep, center stage.)*

UNISON: Let's pledge...

FEMALE DANCER: That on our local stage, we artists will play our roles with bravery and authenticity.

ACTOR/ROOFER: We will improvise on smaller platforms, but promise to perform with excellence and passion.

UNISON: Let's vow together...

AUTHOR: That after a discouraging storm, or lost path, we will not quit.

ACTOR/PATROLMAN and ACTOR/BUSINESSMAN: We will not quit.

TATTOO ARTIST: We will not quit but keep forging the artist's journey.

UNISON: Let's commit...

MALE DANCER: To embrace our highly sensitive nature...

FEMALE DANCER: And keep it from sabotaging our creativity.

BAND TEACHER: Promise yourself that you will value your artistry.

ACTOR/BUSINESSMAN: Not only for self-expression, but for the benefit of your...

UNISON: Community.

ACTOR/PATROLMAN: All of us artists may feel desperately unrehearsed for the roles on our stage.

FEMALE DANCER: But we will show up anyway.

TATTOO ARTIST: Get on the stage, play the role meant for you.

UNISON: On this stage.

BAND TEACHER: Before the final curtain.

MALE DANCER: Dance.

AUTHOR: Write.

TATTOO ARTIST: Draw.

ACTORROOFER/ACTORPATROLMAN/ACTORBUSINESSMAN: Act.

MUSICIAN: Sing.

UNISON: Create.

WOMAN: So you see my fellow artists, there is a stage for you. There is an audience waiting for you to interpret the human experience. *(WOMAN and ACTORS take a bow.)*

NARRATOR: *(Runs in front of group waving his arm with papers in one hand.)* Hey, stage hand, hold that curtain!! This play isn't done. I know it may feel like a finale. But it's not time for the final bow. My script notes have been edited and there is a "choose your own ending."

(NARRATOR shows his script to one of the ACTORS.)

WOMAN: And so dear artist, what parts will you play? What story will you leave with the community? How will your artist journey end? We leave the choosing to you.

BLACKOUT

Use the questions below as prompts to discover the story created in your community.

Cast Call

1. With a group of artists, choose a role in the script above, and read it out loud.
2. Which script lines resonate with you?

3. Where is your stage? Is it too small for you? Too big?
4. Outline your story for the next few months. How can you expand your creative role(s)?
5. Go back to your vision board or statement created after Chapter 4. Choose your own artist finale. What does it look like?
6. Volunteer at your local theater as an actor, or stagehand or usher. How was the audience impacted by the story told on stage? What did you learn about yourself and creativity?

SOURCES

Chapter 1

Elsheimer, Janice, (2001). *The Creative Call.* Colorado Springs, CO: WaterBrook Press.

Seascape at Saintes-Mares https://artsandculture.google.com/asset/seascape-near-les-saintes-maries-de-la-me.

Van Gogh Museum, *The Letters to Theo van Gogh*, Arles, Saturday, August 18, 1888, http://www.vangoghletters.org/vg/letters/let663/letter.html#translation.

Chapter 2

Lamott, Anne, (1994). *Bird by Bird.* New York: Pantheon Books.

Pipher, Mary, (2006). *Writing to Change the World.* New York: Riverhead Books.

Woolf, Virginia, (1929). *A Room of One's Own.* Orlando, FL: Harcourt Brace & Company.

Chapter 3

The Blues Brothers. Directed by John Landis, performances by John Belushi, and Dan Aykroyd, Universal Pictures, 1980.

Aron, Elaine N., PhD, (2013), *The Highly Sensitive Person: How to Thrive When the World Overwhelms You.* New York: Citadel Press.

Chapter 6

Duckworth, Angela, PhD, (2016) *Grit: The Power of Passion and Perseverance.* New York: Scribner Book Co.

Chapter 7

Goleman, D. (2006). *Emotional intelligence: Why it can matter more than IQ* (10th anniversary ed.). New York: Bantam Books
Dierdorff, Erich C., and Robert S. Rubin, March 12, 2015, *Research: We're Not Very Self-Aware, Especially at Work*, https://hbr.org/2015/03/research-were-not-very-self-aware-especially-at-work.

Chapter 8

Strayed, Cheryl, (2012). *Wild: From Lost to Found on the Pacific Crest Trail*. New York: Alfred A. Knopf.
Niffenegger, Audrey, (2009 *Her Fearful Symmetry*. New York: Scribner.
Aldington, Richard, (1929). *Death of a Hero*. Great Britain: Chatto & Windus.
Mitchell, David, (2004). *Cloud Atlas*. New York: Random House.
Gilbert, Elizabeth, (2006). *Eat, Pray, Love: One Woman's Search for Everything Across Italy, India and Indonesia*. New York: Riverhead Books.

Chapter 9

Ratatouille. Directed by Brad Bird, voice performances by Patton Oswalt, Ian Holm, Lou Romano, Janeane Garofalo, Brad Garrett, Peter O'Toole, Brian Dennehy, Peter Sohn, and Will Arnett. Buena Vista Pictures Distribution, 2007.

ACKNOWLEDGMENTS

For artists, creativity happens when working alone and with others. Ideas can formulate when I'm hiking in the mountains of Wyoming or sitting with writers at the library. I am truly thankful for the group of people who gathered on Monday evenings and critiqued the chapters of this book. Their feedback improved my writing skills. The shared laughter enhanced the creative process. Thanks Anna, Merissa, Mary, Dave and John for your belief in this project.

I am honored to share the stories of a few Cheyenne artists: Shane, Leah, Jonathan, Dan, and Amanda. Your willingness to trust me with your creative narrative is a privilege. May your artist journeys inspire the readers as much as you inspired me.

To my Mom, Ruth, I am grateful for her creativity and the endless supply of fabric, paint, piano music, vinyl records, and VHS tapes. Whether it was singing along with the Von Trapp family, or sewing the next Vogue–like outfit, I had the opportunity to create in whatever medium was available.

I'm in awe of how God weaved the threads of my story with artists at Cheyenne Hills Church. Thank you, Dick Young and Galen Huck, for recognizing my leadership and creative gifts. You allowed a space for artists to explore, make mistakes and experience the miracle of co-creating with God to impact our community.

Thank you, God for Your creativity. I am continuously bewildered that You who put rhythm to night and day, paints sunrises and roses, and gives power to words and stories, could bestow creativity on a Wyoming ranch girl. It is a sacred path I cherish. It is a gift I hold with humility. May You get the glory.

Photo by Matthew Idler Photography

René C. McMillen dreamed of being an author and pianist since her childhood days on a ranch in Wyoming. After living in a few other states, she returned to Wyoming to lead artists by developing their creativity and impacting their community. During that time, the unexpected awakening of René's artistic nature added a sharp curve in her journey. She wrestled with her identity—can I call myself a *real* artist? And René questioned the purpose of her creativity—did it even matter in a small town? These questions prompted writing *Abandoning the Road to Hollywood*. René completed a Masters in Communication and Leadership through Gonzaga University.

Connect with René at rcmcmillen.com
Email: rcmcmillen307@gmail.com
Facebook: BrokentoBeauty
Instagram @brokentobeauty374